T0234076

Communications
in Computer and Information Science 605

Commenced Publication in 2007
Founding and Former Series Editors:
Alfredo Cuzzocrea, Dominik Ślęzak, and Xiaokang Yang

Editorial Board

Simone Diniz Junqueira Barbosa
   Pontifical Catholic University of Rio de Janeiro (PUC-Rio),
   Rio de Janeiro, Brazil
Phoebe Chen
   La Trobe University, Melbourne, Australia
Xiaoyong Du
   Renmin University of China, Beijing, China
Joaquim Filipe
   Polytechnic Institute of Setúbal, Setúbal, Portugal
Orhun Kara
   TÜBİTAK BİLGEM and Middle East Technical University, Ankara, Turkey
Igor Kotenko
   St. Petersburg Institute for Informatics and Automation of the Russian
   Academy of Sciences, St. Petersburg, Russia
Ting Liu
   Harbin Institute of Technology (HIT), Harbin, China
Krishna M. Sivalingam
   Indian Institute of Technology Madras, Chennai, India
Takashi Washio
   Osaka University, Osaka, Japan

More information about this series at http://www.springer.com/series/7899

María José Abásolo · Francisco J. Perales
Antoni Bibiloni (Eds.)

Applications and Usability of Interactive TV

4th Iberoamerican Conference, jAUTI 2015
and 6th Congress on Interactive Digital TV, CTVDI 2015
Palma de Mallorca, Spain, October 15–16, 2015
Revised Selected Papers

 Springer

Editors
María José Abásolo
CICPBA - III-LIDI
National University of La Plata
La Plata
Argentina

Antoni Bibiloni
LTIM
University of the Balearic Islands
Palma de Mallorca, Baleares
Spain

Francisco J. Perales
UGIV-IA
University of the Balearic Islands
Palma de Mallorca, Baleares
Spain

ISSN 1865-0929   ISSN 1865-0937   (electronic)
Communications in Computer and Information Science
ISBN 978-3-319-38906-6   ISBN 978-3-319-38907-3   (eBook)
DOI 10.1007/978-3-319-38907-3

Library of Congress Control Number: 2016938665

© Springer International Publishing Switzerland 2016
This work is subject to copyright. All rights are reserved by the Publisher, whether the whole or part of the material is concerned, specifically the rights of translation, reprinting, reuse of illustrations, recitation, broadcasting, reproduction on microfilms or in any other physical way, and transmission or information storage and retrieval, electronic adaptation, computer software, or by similar or dissimilar methodology now known or hereafter developed.
The use of general descriptive names, registered names, trademarks, service marks, etc. in this publication does not imply, even in the absence of a specific statement, that such names are exempt from the relevant protective laws and regulations and therefore free for general use.
The publisher, the authors and the editors are safe to assume that the advice and information in this book are believed to be true and accurate at the date of publication. Neither the publisher nor the authors or the editors give a warranty, express or implied, with respect to the material contained herein or for any errors or omissions that may have been made.

Printed on acid-free paper

This Springer imprint is published by Springer Nature
The registered company is Springer International Publishing AG Switzerland

Preface

The 4th Iberoamerican Conference on Applications and Usability of Interactive TV, jAUTI 2015, and the 6th Congress on Interactive Digital TV, CTVDI 2015, were jointly organized by the Multimedia Information Technologies Laboratory (LTIM) and the Graphics and Computer Vision and Artificial Intelligence Unit (UGIV-IA) of the University of the Balearic Islands, and the Thematic Network on Applications and Usability of Interactive Digital Television (RedAUTI), and were held during June 14–16, 2015, in Palma de Mallorca, Spain.

The RedAUTI is sponsored by the CYTED Ibero American Program of Science and Technology for Development and it consists of 238 researchers from 39 groups from Spain, Portugal, and ten Latin American countries.

These proceedings contain a collection of extended selected papers and invited contributions originally presented at jAUTI 2015–CTVDI 2015 that cover the development and deployment of technologies related to interactive digital TV and their applications. The selection rate was 35 % and the extended selected papers were peer reviewed to assure the high quality of this publication.

March 2016

María José Abásolo
Francisco J. Perales
Antoni Bibiloni

Organization

Program Chairs

María José Abásolo   CICPBA - III-LIDI, National University of La Plata, Argentina
Francisco J. Perales   UGIV-IA, University of the Balearic Islands, Spain
Antoni Bibiloni   LTIM, University of the Balearic Islands, Spain

Program Committee

Jorge Abreu	University of Aveiro, Portugal
Pedro Almeida	University of Aveiro, Portugal
José Luis Arciniegas-Herrera	University of Cauca, Colombia
Sandra Baldassarri	University of Zaragoza, Spain
Ivan Bernal	National Polytechnic School, Ecuador
Sandra Casas	National University of Southern Patagonia, Argentina
Cesar Collazos	University of Cauca, Colombia
Antoni Jaume-i-Capó	University of the Balearic Islands, Spain
Raoni Kulesza	Federal University of Paraíba, Brazil
Cristina Manresa-Yee	University of the Balearic Islands, Spain
Francisco Montero	University of Castilla-La Mancha, Spain
Rita Oliveira	University of Aveiro, Portugal
Douglas Paredes Marquina	University of Los Andes, Venezuela
Miguel Angel Rodrigo-Alonso	University of Córdoba, Spain
Cecilia Sanz	III-LIDI, National University of La Plata, Argentina
Telmo Silva	University of Aveiro, Portugal

From Secondary Screens to Socially-Aware and Immersive Experiences

(Invited Talk)

Pablo Cesar[1,2]

[1] CWI: Centrum Wiskunde & Informatica, Amsterdam, The Netherlands
[2] Delft University of Technology, Delft, The Netherlands
p.s.cesar@cwi.nl

Abstract. Several years ago, first conceptualizations of the usages of the secondary screen in the television environment were proposed. At the time, the real challenge was to convince stakeholders that interactivity was not a threat, but an opportunity. Ten years later, the mass adoption of smaller devices has reshaped the media landscape, truly enabling interactivity while consuming media content at home. What was perceived as hindering the user experience - the second screen - has resulted into an essential companion to the television. Paradoxically, even though key players are investing on secondary screen applications, there are very few successful examples. In this paper we provide an overview of the present state of the art through representative examples and discuss future possibilities and challenges. In particular, we will focus on the importance of immersion, taking into account the surrounding of the users, and of sociability, involving her social network.

Keywords: Social television · Secondary screen · Immersive experiences

1   Socially-Aware and Immersive Experiences

This paper summarizes my keynote talk at the Interactive Digital TV Congress, that took place in Palma de Mallorca (Spain) from 14th to 16th October 2015. The full talk is freely available here: https://www.youtube.com/watch?v=hCGYdg1qbPI.

The following sections provide some relevant scientific resources, in which the keynote talk is based.

1.1   Past

Over a decade ago, we witnessed a revival of the research area of interactive television and online video. A plethora of new ideas and initiatives started reshaping the field. Unlike previous research that mostly focused on the producer concerns, a new generation of researchers started to predict a more interactive role of the user in selecting, producing and distributing content. A good survey about this area of research is this one [4]. Relevant research directions included human-centered television [1] and social television [3, 5]. In those times, first conceptualizations of the usages of the secondary screen in the television environment were as well proposed [2].

1.2 Present

In the past years, the research field of online video and television has significantly evolved moving from the lab to the home, with more robust and reliable solutions available for the masses. Areas of research include content creation and production, content recommendation, connected ecosystem of devices and people, and audience feedback and data analysis [9]. Another relevant research area, still attracting attention, is social television [8]. All these areas and topics are the focus of a recent initiative, the ACM International Conference on Interactive Experiences for Online Video and Television (ACM TVX): http://tvx.acm.org. The conference provides a unique space for the discussion of interdisciplinary research around new and emerging media. From developing an understanding of engagement to informing new ways of creation and consumption for a variety of devices and platforms.

1.3 Future

The number of research topics that will further reshape the media landscape is immense: virtual reality and television (http://www.immersiatv.eu), convergence of broadcast and user generated content for interactive ultra-high definition services (http://cognitus-h2020.eu), multi-sensory experiences (http://www.sussex.ac.uk/schi/). Two very interesting research directions include immersive shared experiences and multi-screen experiences.

The first area of research, immersive shared experiences [6, 7], is the result of the confluence of social networking, multimedia, and computer-mediated interaction. The challenge ahead is to move from current static solutions (e.g., "talking heads") to truly natural and immersive experiences.

The second area of research, multi-screen experiences, is the focus of the EU-funded project 2-IMMERSE. The project is exploring the future of the creation and delivery of shared and personalized multi-screen broadcast and broadband experiences. The project will develop prototype multi-screen experiences for an 'any device' environment. These experiences will merge broadcast and broadband content with the benefits of social media. To deliver the prototypes, 2-IMMERSE will build a platform based on a relatively new specification for television called HbbTV2.0. 2-IMMERSE brings together broadcasters, producers, rights holders, technology companies and universities to design, build and test four prototype experiences involving live performance and sport. More information about the project can be found at: https://2immerse.eu.

Acknowledgements The work presented in this paper was supported by the EU funded H2020 ICT project 2-IMMERSE, under contract 687655.

References

1. Cesar, P., Bulterman, D.C.A., Gomes Soares, L.F.: Human-centered television—directions in interactive digital television research. ACM Trans. Multimedia Comput. Commun. Appl. **4**(4), article 24 (2008)
2. Cesar, P., Bulterman, D.C.A., Jansen, J.: Leveraging the user impact: an architecture for secondary screens usage in an interactive television environment. Springer Multimedia Syst. J. **15**(3), 127–142 (2009)
3. Cesar, P., Geerts, D., Chorianopoulos, K. (eds.): Social Interactive Television: Immersive Shared Experiences and Perspectives. IGI Global Publishing, Hershey (2009)
4. Cesar, P., Chorianopoulos. K.: The evolution of TV systems, content, and users towards interactivity. Found. Trends Hum.-Comput. Interact. **2**(4), 279–373 (2009)
5. Cesar, P., Geerts, D.: Understanding social TV: a survey. In: Proceedings of the Networked and Electronic Media Summit (NEM Summit), pp. 27–29 (2011)
6. Cesar, P., Kaiser, R., Ursu. M.F.: Toward connected shared experiences. IEEE Comput. **47**(7), 86–89 (2014)
7. Cesar, P.: Immersive shared experiences. In: Proceedings of the International Workshop on Immersive Media Experiences, p. 19 (2015)
8. Cesar P., Geerts, D.: Social interaction design for online video and television. In: Nakatsu, R., Rauterberg, M., Ciancarini, P. (eds.) Handbook of Digital Games and Entertainment Technologies. Springer, Germany (2016)
9. Obrist, M., Cesar, P., Geerts, D., Bartindale, T., Churchill, E.F.: Online video and interactive TV experiences. ACM Interact. **22**(5), 32–37 (2015)

Contents

IDTV User Experience

Audiovisual Accessibility

Second Screen Applications
Immersive TV. Short Papers

Enriching and Engaging Linear Television: Findings and Learnings with HbbTV Second Screen Applications

Joost Negenman[1], Susanne Heijstraten[1], Jeroen Vanattenhoven[2(✉)], and David Geerts[2]

[1] NPO R&D, Bart de Graaffweg 2, 1217 ZL Hilversum, The Netherlands
{joost.negenman,susanne.heijstraten}@npo.nl
[2] Meaningful Interactions Lab (mintlab), KU Leuven – iMinds, Parkstraat 45 bus 3605, 3000 Leuven, Belgium
{jeroen.vanattenhoven,david.geerts}@soc.kuleuven.be

Abstract. In this article we present findings from a research project on novel TV applications using second screens. We introduce new ways of enriching and engaging linear television by using HbbTV services in combination with second screen applications. HbbTV stands for Hybrid Broadcast Broadband TV, and focuses on bringing together the TV and the online world. Our goal was to make the social viewing experience more compelling by incorporating second screen functionality into TV formats. Our findings, obtained via substantial iterative user involvement, are the outcome of participation in the European TV-RING project, with the aim to develop and stimulate HbbTV within Europe.

Keywords: HbbTv · Second screen · Interactive television · Social TV

1 Introduction

In September 2015, Tim Cook stated *"The TV experience itself hasn't changed that much in decades, in fact the television experience has been virtually standing still while innovation has been thriving in the mobile space..."* [1]. This illustrates that there is not a lot of innovation around TV. However, in the online and mobile domains substantial changes have taken place. Whereas the linear television world is built around user needs, viewer's day-care and know-how of linear programming, the online world is unlimited and not time-critical. Linear TV viewing sometimes meets online via for example second screen interactivity or direct references from linear programs to more related video-on-demand (VoD) content or extra or follow up program information, which can be found either in a Smart TV app or in online applications. These two examples show how these two worlds meet and re-enforce each other; these are examples of linear enrichment. We created a new and innovative way of watching television: we focused on allowing viewers to play against each other in their living room. The platform we developed, makes it possible to play along with a second screen application that interacts and aggregates scores on the HbbTV content layer on a central TV screen, creating an engaged social in-house experience. It becomes fun again and social to watch and play together in a domestic setting.

© Springer International Publishing Switzerland 2016
M.J. Abásolo et al. (Eds.): jAUTI 2015/CTVDI 2015, CCIS 605, pp. 3–8, 2016.
DOI: 10.1007/978-3-319-38907-3_1

2   Related Work

Most of the Social TV related work, has focused on supporting viewers at different locations [2]. An example of such an application is the MarathOn Multiscreen application, which allows users to "view, share and curate amateur and professional video footage of a community marathon event" [3]. FANFEEDS is an application that uses information from a person's social network to feed a companion app for a specific TV show [4]. As such, the social network is able to comment on a show. Afterwards, someone in this network who hasn't seen this show can watch it and view the generated comments at the original timing during the show. Many TV shows have a second screen application that makes it possible to play along, or to look up related information [5]. This is in many cases an individual experience with sometimes a social media extension. In contrast, the contribution of this paper lies in the fact that we focus on supporting collocated users. We achieve this by making use of the second-screen devices people are already using in front of the TV to check their emails or engage with social networks [6]. By creating second-screen applications for a specific TV show, we draw these viewers' attention back to the show. Furthermore, our aim was to stimulate the user experience, more specifically, the social and competitive experience.

3   Methodology

In this article we report on the field study results for three TV shows and their respective second-screen applications: The National IQ Quiz, the Eurovision Song contest, and the quiz "Een tegen 100" (Dutch for "1 against 100"). We gathered a user panel, composed of approximately 40 households, with three to five people, individuals or couples (age: 4–64y). During the 30 months of the project, this user panel was updated and reviewed several times. For the field studies, participants used the second-screen applications during the broadcast, after which they were asked to complete an online questionnaire about their experience. For this, they received an incentive in the form of a six-month subscription to NL Ziet, a Dutch VoD service with HD content from public and commercial broadcasters. Additional incentives were foreseen for the evaluating each application.

3.1   Use Cases

The first use case is The National IQ test (A Test The Nation based format), a Dutch TV show with a second screen application that can be used to play along. This program exists for almost 15 years and people in the show and at home are challenged by 60 multiple choice questions that measures their IQ. In 2015 there were around 1.5 million viewers and 125,000 users who played along the second screen app. Most of the viewers were 35y or older, with a majority even 65y and older. However, the use of the second screen applications is the heaviest in the youngest group of users, the group between 13y and 19y. The other two use cases (Eurovision Song context and Een tegen 100) allowed collocated viewers to play against each other, along with the TV program. To achieve such interaction, we introduce questions from TV-shows, polls, ask people to react tot statements, which can be responded to by users in the living room on their personal second screen (see Figs. 1 and 2). The second screen app players view their individual results presented on the first screen, the central TV. The latter is important since we found that viewers rather have this part on the common screen in order to have a more social experience; otherwise all players are constantly looking down on their own screen (individually).

Fig. 1. Each player activates the second screen app and creates its own digital profile (like a picture or avatar) or gets one assigned (example from "Een tegen 100").

Fig. 2. On the second screen app or from the TV-show the question appears that must be answered. On TV's HbbTV layer the answer of each player is displayed, using signaling colors such as green (good answer) and red (wrong answer) – example from "Eurosong". (Color figure online)

The score is updated after each round, encouraging competition and social interaction in the living room. If there are more than four people playing along viewers can be divided into two groups (A and B) who compete against each other. It's also possible to display the aggregated outcomes of all other second screen players of the show in different cut outs, such as region or country.

3.2 Field Study

For the National IQ Quiz evaluation, we also asked participants to complete online questionnaires after using the second screen application at home during a live broadcast. Six questionnaires were completed in this evaluation. This questionnaire was based on the Social Presence in Gaming Questionnaire in order to investigate the social interaction aspects of collocated games [7]. For the Eurovision Song contest application, two volunteering households (no incentive) were recruited; one in Spain and one in The Netherlands. In total, 11 participants took part, 6 women and 5 men. Their age ranged between 24 and 64 years old (average = 37.5y). These participants used the second screen application during the broadcast of the finals of the Eurovision Song contest in May, 2015. Hereafter, they were asked to complete an online questionnaire, of which ten were completed. The questionnaires were designed to inquire about the usability, user experience, social experience, social interaction, and the extent to which the second screen application might have distracted participants from the show. The methodology for the "Een tegen 100" quiz show application was similar.

3.3 Technical Platform

The implementation for HbbTV is a web extension of the existing real time platform (Play Now!) created by the Hilversum based company Angry Bytes, primarily used for massive real-time interaction on companion screens. We ensured that the companion screen runs in all browsers on most desktops, tablets and mobiles. The platform uses websockets (with fallbacks for older browsers) to the Amazon Elastic Cloud (EC2). The HbbTV extension shows all quiz data gathered on connected devices in the same local network (sharing a Public IP address) on the HbbTV web layer. Participants in the living room who selected the multiplayer option can see what their peers are doing on television.

4   Results

4.1 National IQ Quiz

The following insights were gathered via user interviews and questionnaires:

- The more people in a household are involved watching a show, the greater their desire to play together.
- Playing on the second screen can – in specific circumstances – distract people from the first screen (the TV).
- Some viewers experienced usability issues logging in and creating a profile on the second screen application.

- At this stage in the application, viewers are still playing individually; there is no competition between household members.

4.2 Eurosong and "Een Tegen 100"

To optimize this first screen experience and the second screen application, we first thoroughly analyzed how people are watching television at home [8, 9], engaged many users in prototyping and ideation sessions in order to generate novel designs, and evaluated the newly developed concepts in field trials [10]. Our most important insights are:

- Allow the TV show to be dependent on the results from the second screen results for a higher audience engagement.
- People using second screens can be distracted from the main show from time to time. To minimize this, confine the game's decisive moments to brief and well-chosen moments during the TV show.
- As is the case with most games, rewards and incentives causes viewers to experience more competition.
- People prefer playing against people they know.
- Competition itself is a useful element to increase engagement.
- Make sure the application is very easy to use. This means making procedures such as logging in very minimal.
- Try to publish most of the information on the TV screen itself (scores, call-to-actions). This makes the experience more social as every player is not looking down on his or her own second screen.

5 Conclusion and Future Work

We created a new innovative HbbTV service. We added value in watching TV with second screen play-along in a household- or another closed network setting. For future work, we plan to extend this experience among households or friends via social networks such as Twitter and Facebook. We can demonstrate this application in a real live setting, with several viewers playing along with their own personal second screen device. The audience will be challenged to critically think along in how this TV extension may open possibilities for TV formats or social interaction.

Acknowledgements. The research leading to these results was carried out in the TV-RING project (EC Grant Agreement ICT PSP-325209). More information about the project can be found on http://www.tvring.eu.

References

1. Moynihan, T.: The New Apple TV Is Siri's Time to Shine. http://www.wired.com/2015/09/new-apple-tv-siris-time-shine/
2. Cesar, P., Geerts, D.: Past, present, and future of social TV: A categorization. In: 2011 IEEE Consumer Communications and Networking Conference (CCNC), pp. 347–351 (2011)

 3. Anstead, E., Benford, S., Houghton, R.: MarathOn multiscreen: group television watching and interaction in a viewing ecology. In: Proceedings of the 19th ACM Conference on Computer-Supported Cooperative Work & Social Computing, pp. 405–417. ACM, New York (2016)
 4. Basapur, S., Mandalia, H., Chaysinh, S., Lee, Y., Venkitaraman, N., Metcalf, C.: FANFEEDS: evaluation of socially generated information feed on second screen as a TV show companion. In: Proceedings of the 10th European Conference on Interactive Tv and Video, pp. 87–96. ACM, New York (2012)
 5. Nandakumar, A., Murray, J.: Companion apps for long arc TV series: supporting new viewers in complex storyworlds with tightly synchronized context-sensitive annotations. In: Proceedings of the 2014 ACM International Conference on Interactive Experiences for TV and Online Video, pp. 3–10. ACM, New York (2014)
 6. Vanattenhoven, J., Geerts, D.: Second-Screen Use in the Home: an Ethnographic Study. Presented at the Bridging people, places & platforms: Proceedings EuroITV 2012, July 1 (2012)
 7. de Kort, Y.A., IJsselsteijn, W.A., Poels, K.: Digital games as social presence technology: Development of the Social Presence in Gaming Questionnaire (SPGQ). In: Proceedings of PRESENCE, pp. 195–203 (2007)
 8. Vanattenhoven, J., Geerts, D.: Broadcast, video-on-demand, and other ways to watch television content: a household perspective. In: Proceedings of the ACM International Conference on Interactive Experiences for TV and Online Video, pp. 73–82. ACM, New York (2015)
 9. Geerts, D., Leenheer, R., De Grooff, D., Negenman, J., Heijstraten, S.: In front of and behind the second screen: viewer and producer perspectives on a companion app. In: Proceedings of the 2014 ACM International Conference on Interactive Experiences for TV and Online Video, pp. 95–102. ACM, New York (2014)
10. Leenheer, R., Geerts, D., Vanattenhoven, J.: Learning lessons for second screen from board games. In: Proceedings of the ACM International Conference on Interactive Experiences for TV and Online Video, pp. 143–148. ACM, New York (2015)

TV-RING and ImmersiaTV: Present and Future of Television

Marc Aguilar[✉], Pau Pamplona, and Sergi Fernández

Media Internet Area, i2CAT Foundation, Gran Capità 2-4, Nexus I building, 203,
08034 Barcelona, Spain
{marc.aguilar,pau.pamplona,sergi.fernandez}@i2cat.net

Abstract. In this paper we present our results from a research project on multi-camera HbbTV applications, the TV-RING project, and situate these results as part of a broader push towards the development of innovative media experiences for TV audiences. The main lessons learned in the framework of this project are outlined, with special attention paid to principles of usability, insights on the user experience, and recommendations for the selection of multicamera content. These results were generated as the output of a user-centered design and experimentation process, involving requirements elicitation, iterative prototyping and large-scale live pilots. Finally, we sketch how immersive media can address current issues as regards the user experience raised by TV-RING, and introduce related ongoing work in the ImmersiaTV project on broadcast omnidirectional video.

Keywords: Connected TV · Hbbtv · User evaluation · Multicamera · Immersive TV

1 Introduction

In the last years, the mission of i2CAT Foundation's Media Internet Area has been centered on the development of innovative audiovisual experiences. In the framework of the TV-RING project, the focus has been placed on the user-centered development of adaptive-streaming, MPEG-DASH-enabled multicamera HbbTV applications. In the upcoming ImmersiaTV project, the focus of work will shift to immersive television, an emerging paradigm which holds the promise to revolutionize the TV viewing experience. This position paper presents an overview of the main outcomes of the TV-RING project's multicamera pilot, and attempts to delineate the relevance and continuity of its research in the ImmersiaTV project.

2 The TV-RING Project Multicamera Pilot

The multicamera pilot application, developed by TV-RING partner Televisió de Catalunya (TVC), consists of two main scenarios or areas of work. Firstly, a VoD service of content that can be accessed interactively from one or two different points of view or 'renditions' and secondly, accessing multiple renditions on a live TV show. Content is

© Springer International Publishing Switzerland 2016
M.J. Abásolo et al. (Eds.): jAUTI 2015/CTVDI 2015, CCIS 605, pp. 9–14, 2016.
DOI: 10.1007/978-3-319-38907-3_2

accessed using MPEG-DASH in all cases, allowing for seamless and instantaneous timeline shifting in the first case and actual live content in the second case. All contents are offered in three different qualities, ranging from the 7 Mbps at HD, to an intermediate 5 Mbps, to 3 Mbps at SD using MPEG-DASH.

The application is made up of different screens. It is mainly composed of a screen with two lists of contents, one with a live content and the other with the VOD content. The user can interact with the application using the remote control of the HbbTV-enabled TV set device, enabling the user to select content, control video playback and specify video renditions. Finally, in the start menu, the user has option to display help screen by pressing the blue button on the remote control. Based on insights from the preliminary user evaluation, the application was enhanced with a second screen functionality to allow users to control the HbbTV application using a mobile device as remote control. In the following figure (Fig. 1), a workflow of the application can be found to better describe the different GUI interactions. For further details on the test application, readers are kindly referred to the bibliography [1–3].

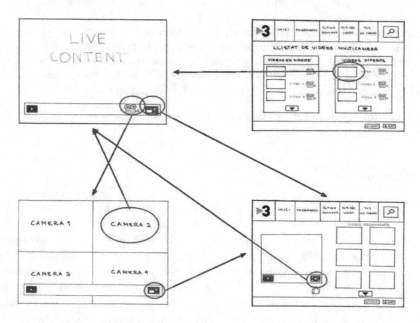

Fig. 1. Multicamera pilot application basic interaction pattern

As delineated in the piloting plan, a sequence of tests was carried out over a thirteen-month period [4]. This constituted the final phase of a user-centered design process which had previously involved users in two rounds of requirements analysis and three iterations of prototype refinement. First, four small-sample controlled pilots were executed from December 2014 to June 2015. This phase involved twenty households in the town of Gurb, in central Catalonia. Each household was given an HbbTV 1.5 device capable to play MPEG-DASH and last generation services. Test users were connected to a monitored fibre network of 100 Mb/s using a local controlled CDN, from which detailed analytics could be monitored. At this stage, the goal was to fine-tune the usability of the test application, sort out any outstanding technical issues, and obtain market data on the most attractive contents for users to be used in larger experiments. The contents for these tests were a singing contest show, a special news report on the Spanish local elections, and two football matches.

This first phase of controlled-sample pilot tests set the stage for the two large-scale open pilots. A preparatory pilot was carried out in September, with news coverage of the Catalan national day rally, to ensure the successful deployment of the envisioned live pilots. The selected contents for the live pilots were two FC Barcelona football matches in September and November 2015. These open live pilots were followed by an audience of about 4000 and 6200 TV devices which accessed the project's HbbTV application (see Fig. 2), representing an audience of thousands of users interacting with the offered multicamera services. Extensive data was obtained on the patterns of usage of the application, technical performance parameters and several metrics of user satisfaction. An in-depth analysis of these data has yielded rich information on HbbTV market penetration potential, models of user segmentation and clustering, and analytics on the user's behavior in real-life settings.

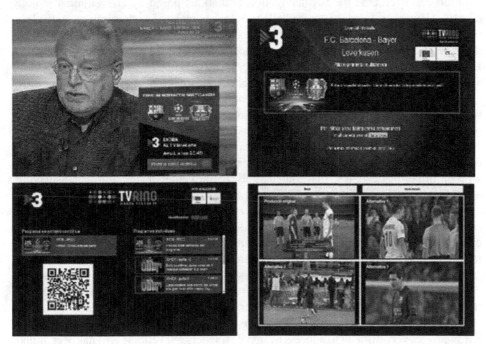

Fig. 2. Screenshots of application during open live pilot tests

Finally, three batteries of in-lab technical tests were carried out as well in November and December 2015. These tests were designed to test the performance of the TVC application across a range of TV devices, to evaluate the performance of the MPEG-DASH encoder, and to determine experimentally the impact of hardware performance on latency and user satisfaction.

3 Lessons Learned

Multicamera content can be attractive for audiences under certain usability conditions and for certain programs. Nevertheless, there are constraints from a user-centric point of view that may limit its generalization if not properly addressed by HbbTV application designers.

Early on during the user evaluation activities, it was found that traditional remote controls offer very poor usability for users accustomed to more agile handheld device navigations. Several approaches to replace or complement the traditional remote control have been successfully implemented, such as speech and gesture recognition controls [5]. In the TV-RING project multicamera pilot, a Second Screen solution was tested on field trials. The results obtained give weight to the hypothesis that a Second Screen solution can overcome the app navigation limitations posed by conventional remote controls. However, there are some challenges to the uptake of such solutions, as the less technically-savvy users (which usually coincide with older cohorts) are held back by the lack of compatible handhelds in some households and the need to link the devices. Easing the Second Screen – TV linking process, for example with QR codes and visual step-by-step instructions, is paramount to accelerate uptake.

A number of general usability recommendations for the design of HbbTV applications emerge from the prototype refinement and live piloting phases. These include offering very agile navigations, ensuring consistency in commands by using color codes (i.e. red means go back, green means go forward), making explicit to the user the function of every button (forward, back to main screen, exit app), limiting clutter in the screen with minimalistic designs so that content is always the center of attention, and displaying a machine reaction for every user action [6].

A significant finding is that hardware performance problems have a serious impact on the user experience. Users may display some patience with waiting while loading contents and slight degradations in video quality, but are not so understanding with instances in which they feel their TVs take an excessive amount of time to process their requests. More specifically, hardware delays above the 5–6 s threshold were found to produce frustration in most test users. This frustration increases progressively as delays become longer, quickly deteriorating the user experience. Delays above the 8–10 s mark were considered not acceptable by all test users. Performance problems attributable to hardware are very difficult to address by app developers. Nevertheless, it has been found that their negative impact on the user experience can be minimized by the simple expedient of adding any indication of "task in progress" for the user (i.e. a completion bar, a "wait…" sign), and this reassures the user and may compel her to "stay tuned" [7].

Content selection is critical for the success of a multicamera HbbTV application. Programs in which the relevant action may happen simultaneously in several locations are the best picks for multicamera content. Sports such as football, basketball or tennis, and racing events like the Formula One or MotoGP competitions have been identified as particularly suitable contents for multicamera. Other kinds of contents such as special informative events (i.e. demonstrations, election days) and song contests were piloted during the course of the TV-RING project. The audience's reaction to these programs was fairly positive as well. Nevertheless, a lesser level of interest was detected, as many users did not see the value of multicamera services for those kinds of programs vis-à-vis the broadcast content produced by an experienced audiovisual producer.

4 Beyond the Current User Experience: The ImmersiaTV Project

Immersive TV has the potential to overcome these limitations by bringing to audiences a radically novel experience. The majority of European TV consumers already watch TV programs in a multi-display environment. Second screens —mostly smartphones, tablets or laptops— are generally used to check information not directly related to the events in the TV content being watched. As a result, the attention of the audience is generally divided between these different streams of information. Broadcasters have tried (like in TV-RING) to orchestrate all these different rendering platforms to complement each other consistently. However, their success is limited, and this is due, at least in part, to the very different formats in which information is delivered (web-based texts, mobile apps, hybrid apps, traditional broadcast television, etc.).

The ImmersiaTV project will create new forms of digital storytelling and broadcast production that, by putting omnidirectional video at the center of the creation, production and distribution of broadcast content, delivers an all-encompassing experience that integrates the specificities of immersive displays, and the feeling of "being there", within the contemporary living room. We propose a new form of broadcast omnidirectional video that offers end-users a coherent audiovisual experience across head mounted displays, second screens and the traditional TV set, instead of having their attention divided across them. This new experience will seamlessly integrate with and further augment traditional TV and second screen consumer habits. In other terms: the audience will still be able to watch TV sitting on their couch, or tweet comments about it. However, by putting omnidirectional content at the center of the creation, production and distribution processes, the audience will also be able to use immersive displays to feel like being inside the audiovisual stream.

5 Conclusions

This paper has discussed the work performed in the framework of the TV-RING project in the field of multicamera HbbTV applications, and outlined the main conclusions learned as regards the user's preferences, experience and behavior with such services. Multicamera services have been well received by audiences, provided that these are offered via user-friendly apps, run on well-performing devices, and supported by adequate contents. These lessons will inform the work to be done in the ImmersiaTV project. In this Horizon 2020 initiative, which started January 2016, an attempt is being made to redefine TV viewing by bringing an immersive experience to the user's household.

Acknowledgements. The research for this paper has been partially funded by the CIP-PSP Programme under grant agreement 325209.

References

1. Vogl, A., et al.: D3.3.1 Service Implementation Report. Public report, TV-RING project (2014). http://www.TV-RING.eu/documentation/deliverables/
2. Baumann, F., et al.: D3.3.2. Services and Applications. Public report, TV-RING project (2014)
3. Pujals, D., et al.: D3.4 Description of Technical Pilot Infrastructures. Public report, TV-RING project (2015)
4. Pamplona, P., et al.: D4.2. Pilot Execution Report. Public report, TV-RING project (2015)
5. Vanattenhoven, J., Geerts, D., De Grooff, D.: Television experience insights from HbbTV. In: Proceedings of 2nd International Workshop on Interactive Content Consumption at TVX 2014, Newcastle, UK, pp. 32–34 (2014)
6. Glaser, S., et al.: D3.2 Intermediate Evaluation Report. Public report, TV-RING project (2014)
7. Vanattenhoven, J., et al.: D4.3. Evaluation Results. Public report, TV-RING project (2016)

Video Consumption Development Tools

Implementing the Complete Chain to Distribute Interactive Multi-stream Multi-view Real-Time Life Video Content

Marc Codina[1,2]($\boxtimes$), Jordi Gonzalez[1,2], Antoni Barroso[1,2], Jordi Caball[1,2], and Jordi Carrabina[1,2]

[1] CEPHIS, Edifici Q, Universitat Autnoma de Barcelona,
08193 Bellaterra, Spain
{marc.codina,jordi.carrabina}@uab.cat
[2] VSN, Parc Audiovisual de Catalunya, Ctra. BV-1274 Km.1,
08225 Terrassa, Spain

Abstract. This paper presents the development of a complete end-to-end solution for the broadcast of Multi-Stream Multi-view Real-Time Life Video Content that makes use of the new chips implementing full-spectrum receiver chips that can decode up to 16 TV channels simultaneously and pass them to the video processing chips of the Set-Top Boxes. Managing that complex video content from a user's perspective requires adding interactive ways to increase user experience.Interactivity can either be directly managed on the main screen through the Set Top Box or on a Second Screen that is wireless connected to the Set Top Box. Several underlying technologies have been implemented that involve: the production head ends that include adding time stamps in the protocol for synchronizing streams and views; the GStreamer technology for scaling videos in real-time and the responsive design used for the 2nd screen apps management.

Keywords: Multi-stream Multi-view video broadcast · Full spectrum receiver · Set top box · GStreamer · Second screen

1 Introduction

The set-top box (STB) is the primary entry point into the digital home for television services including cable TV, satellite TV and IPTV. This device has evolved beyond its historical role as a simple black box sitting on top of a large TV set into a device that supports a variety of functions, notably interactive television applications. Another interesting development is the concept of residential gateway, which is a complex device capable of delivering multiple services to the home, including video, voice and data(sensors, actuators, security, payment, etc.). Figure 1 shows the evolution of the STB concept.

© Springer International Publishing Switzerland 2016
M.J. Abásolo et al. (Eds.): jAUTI 2015/CTVDI 2015, CCIS 605, pp. 17–25, 2016.
DOI: 10.1007/978-3-319-38907-3_3

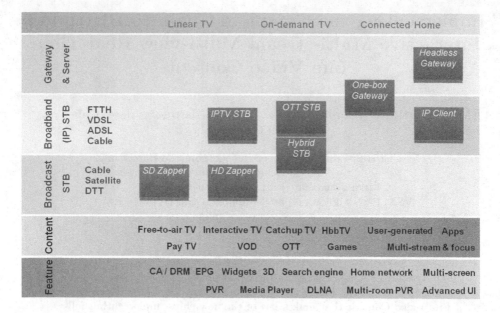

Fig. 1. STB evolution

Both the set-top box and the residential gateway can be combined into a unified platform to deliver the same rich experience to multiple users in different rooms. The concept of application gateway is related to the this extended platform that allows seamless integration and access of diverse heterogeneous devices together with multiple applications. In order to develop that concept, the european project APPSGATE [1] was set up for the period 2012-1015. This new platform, which offers the prospect of unprecedented business opportunities, is the focus of the project and includes many different home-related applications.

The core of the Appsgate project was intended to develop the HW, FW, SW and apps related to the new generation of STB capable of tuning simultaneously multiple streams of video at the same time and send them over home network to different multimedia devices. This is a completely new set of features compared with the current available technologies and justifies the concept of home gateway.

The list of addressed applications is particularly long and includes:

– Entertainment (games, HD video conference, social networking, interactive TV and video on demand for multiple users).
– Home automation (home control, safety, security and surveillance, energy management).
– Personal Health (telemedicine, chronic disease management, ambient assisted living, wellness).

To be able to tune several TV channels simultaneously, we used a new silicon technology based on the so-called wide-band tuner technology (also called Full-spectrum Receiver), initially developed for cable access, but now expanding to satellite and in the coming years to terrestrial digital broadcast access as well. The wide-band tuner [2,3] behaves as if 8, 16 or even more tuners were available simultaneously, providing the home with a fat data pipe.

At the same time, media content consumption is being redefined somehow. As mentioned on AdAge [4]: Big screen TVs will more and more be used for tentpole, live viewing for the types of programming that must be consumed live, including sporting events, awards shows, election and disaster coverage. The big screen will also be used to view can't-miss series with friends and family (...). During these relatively few and far-between video events, tablets will become co-viewing screens, allowing us to comment, rate, and share the experience with others or to look away when the action wanes.

Set-top-boxes are commonly designed to operate a single display. A paradigm change is happening where set-top-boxes are also fulfilling concurrent needs, transforming our shared TV display into a smart provider of social and emotional experience, and accompanying our Wi-Fi connected mobile displays into much personal interactive feature-rich platforms, while providing both with access to a common apps base, data base and media base. Furthermore, this fundamental connectivity is being complemented by either wireless or wired protocols and applications related to the home environment such as those related to entertainment, home automation and personal health.

The challenge of taking the highest profit of these new platforms is a major concern for both for engineers and user experience (UX) designers. Engineers shall provide means to distribute video streams of high quality to displays of different sizes in the home network, through either a cable (i.e. ethernet) or a Wi-Fi link, and bridge that main connectivity with other protocols (Bluetooth incl. BLE-, Z-Wave, zigbee, etc.). They should also implement the adaptable user interface software libraries that UX designers use to implement applications that will run on both the TV connected set-top-boxes and on other displays in the home network [5] that can display media content either independently or connected to the main display as second screens for monitoring and managing the content. In this case, content synchronization is needed and it should be platform independent. Web technologies already allow such synchronization [6].

The rest of the paper is organized as follows: Sect. 2 shows the global architecture; Sect. 3 describes our implementation; Sect. 4 presents our results and we conclude the work in Sect. 5.

2   System Architecture

In the framework of the APPSGATE project, the SW architecture of the Multi-Stream Multi-view framework is shown in Fig. 2. This SW architecture is supported by a set of 2 complex development boards plus the standard commercial production (from VSN) and consumption (TV, tablet, smartphone) devices. One board contains the gateway tuner that decodes and sends MPEG-2 streams to the STB platform that manages the multi-stream video and related interactivity.

End-users can choose from different views while watching a live event "channel". Several video streams will be offered and they can be played simultaneously

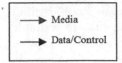

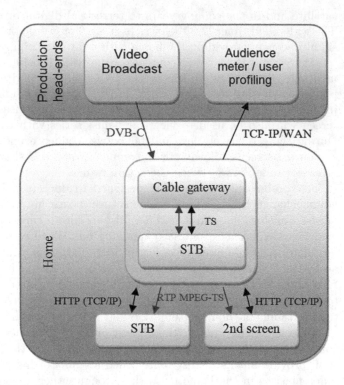

Fig. 2. General application architecture

and synchronously in a composition on the TV set. Besides, those video streams can be also played on a second screen. This provides the end-users with further interactivity resulting in a better experience of viewing live events.

In our proposal, the composition of the video streams in the screen will be defined by the channel manager or by expert users using the different user interfaces available in the AppsGate platform (remote control, tablet, gesture, voice, etc.).

The behavior of the user will be used to measure audience. Audience measurements will be sent back to the production head-ends where user profiling tools can be applied to cluster users to further provide them with more adapted and personalized content.

3   Implementation

This section describes the implementation details of the components that we built for our implementation by using C, Python and Java on the related platforms and second screen devices. Our implementation manages the cable gateway with the full spectrum receiver tuner, capable of tune in 16 channels simultaneously. The STB manages requests from users to tune and synchronize channels

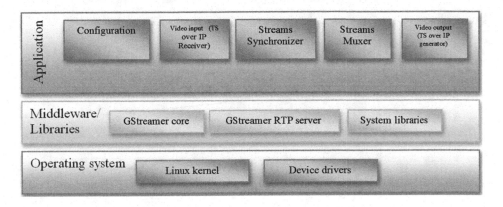

Fig. 3. Multistream dispatcher stack

and send them to the requested device. Although it is possible to tune up to 16 channels simultaneously, for usability and performance reasons we selected to handle 4 HD and 4 SD channels simultaneously. We limited our implementations to 480 and 720p video due to the performance of our test equipment but the system is prepared to support 1080p.

Multi-stream dispatcher is the service responsible for obtaining streams from the gateway tuner. The streams are received in MPEG-TS over IP using RTP over UDP. The following modules, depicted in Fig. 3, are part of the Multi-stream dispatcher:

- Dispatcher service. Processes commands received from the multistream player
- Tuner. Request channels to the gateway-tuner.
- Streams synchronization. The tuned streams are synchronized in this module.
- Streams compositor. Composes the streams requested by the dispatcher service and generates a new stream available for the streaming service module.
- Streaming service. Sends the synchronized streams to the multistream player using RTP over UDP protocols.

Our SW implementation uses Gstreamer [7] (both its core and some plugins) for tasks such as demux, synchronize and compose the multiple streams received and also GStreamer RTP server to send the synchronized streams to the Multistream player module.

The player module has an internal clock that generates time signals for synchronous playback. The reproduction of the various streams will be based on these time signals. Each time signal has to play the corresponding samples of all streams. The corresponding sample time is determined by the time stamp.

In order to ensure that all data streams are available at the time they are needed to be reproduced, it is necessary to use buffering techniques. Those smart buffers store samples and plays then according to their corresponding time stamp, as shown in Fig. 4. Buffer size is empirically set based on the estimated maximum time difference between all data available.

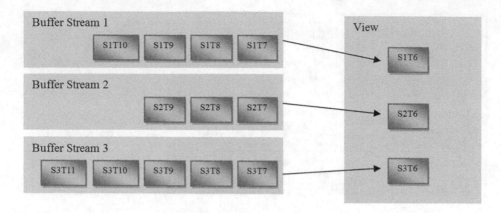

Fig. 4. Buffer queues at T6

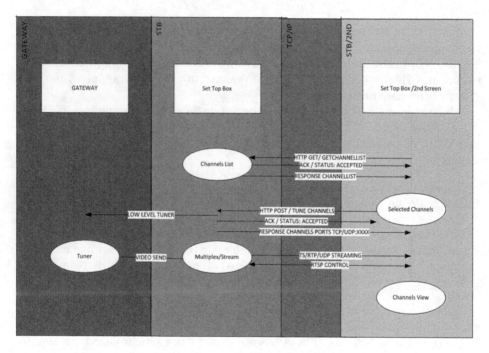

Fig. 5. Communication schema gateway, STB and STB/2ndScreen

Interactivity has been implemented using a web server to handle the user requests concerning channel management. This web server has been implemented using Django REST [8]. In our implementation, control devices request the list of all available channels that users will be able to select. If these channels are not currently decoded, the system will order its selection to the tuner. This is the classical high latency mode.

Fig. 6. Android app with channel menu and live stream

Complementary, if the channel is already being decoded, and therefore is in the STB platform, any management operation on it will be fast, thus producing a low latency switching operation. Furthermore, we have been able to display several channels (1HD + 4SD) on the same screen so that the selection of the one that is in HD from the 4 in SD is really very fast due to the fact that all of them are already in the STB memory.

This allows improving the user experience both concerning fast response (low-latency) and personalization (i.e. camera or view selection) that is quite desirable for real-time events such as sports (i.e. motor bikes to select with motorbike to view).

Figure 5 represent communication schema between devices, STB and cable gateway. HTTP Post and Get are used to transfer information between devices and STB. When the channel is selected, the STB communicates with the cable gateway tuner and begins to decode, synchronize and send the requested stream.

An Android application has been developed for the second screen management. Using integrated Android API we were able to request the server for channel list and show the channels and views selected by the user on the screen. When a channel is selected, the video starts to be played. It is also possible to send that video to another screen. The user can enter a new IP address and the video will be stopped on the android device and continue being played at its new destination. Other versions of the android app where implemented to create a personal video composition in which users can select the channels they want to watch and be able to show the 4 streams multiview composition on the android device.

4   Results

Figure 6 shows two screenshots of the Android application developed to play a channel selected from the available channel list. The image is synchronized at the STB before being displayed at the Android device. If we have a TV playing the same channel, the image will be synchronized in a few seconds. We tested

Fig. 7. Android app with multiview videos from STB and online stream

that the synchronization between TV, tablet and a channel send to a new device is being synchronized correctly.

Figure 7 shows the screenshot of a second Android application developed. On this one, users are able to create a composition of different channels and play at the same time a video on streaming from Internet. On this test, we correct validated the performance on streaming multi-view videos to the Android platform.

5   Conclusion

The main conclusion of our work is that we reach to develop a complete chain to distribute interactive multi-stream multi-view synchronized real-time life video content. This has been possible thanks to the evolution of the hardware platforms that allowed obtaining multiple channels simultaneously from the same input signal by using the full spectrum receiver capabilities. That piece of hardware is key to complete the complete chain composed of production, distribution and user platform front-end. This allowed us to develop new models for multi-view interactivity at either the main display screen (STB + SmartTV) or using portable platforms (tablets, smartphones) that can act as second screens to manage the content selection on the main screen, through their WiFi connection.

These results will evolve together with the evolution of the integration density that produces every day more integrated silicon platforms that allows moving from the classical Set Top Box concept to the new Home Gateway.

Acknowledgments. Authors would like to thank the support for the ST team in APPSGATE, Jean-Christophe Pont and Jerome Maupay and also from other colleagues at VSN and colleagues from Fluendo concerning initial discussions on their open framework. Authors would like to thank also CDTI for funding the project APPSGATE at Spanish level with the project reference IDI-20130632.

References

1. APPSGATE Project. http://www.appsgate-catrene.org/
2. Le Duc, H., Jabbour, C., Desgreys, P., Jamin, O.: A fully digital background calibration of timing skew in undersampling TI-ADC. In: 2014 IEEE 12th International New Circuits and Systems Conference (NEWCAS), pp. 53–56. IEEE, June 2014
3. NXP TDA18264HB Full Spectrum Transceiver. http://www.nxp.com/products/tv_and_stb_front_ends/silicon_tuners/cable_and_terrestrial_silicon_tuners/TDA18264HB.html
4. How Tablets Will Soon Top TVs For Most Video Viewing. http://adage.com/article/digitalnext/tablets-top-tvs-video-viewing/233039/
5. Itzkovitch, A.: Designing for Context: the Multiscreen Ecosystem, Smashing Magazine (2012). http://uxmag.com/articles/designing-for-context-the-multiscreen-ecosystem
6. Rodriguez-Alsina, A., Talavera, G., Orero, P., Carrabina, J.: Subtitle synchronization across multiple screens and devices. Sensors **12**(7), 8710–8731 (2012)
7. GStreamer, open source multimedia framework. http://gstreamer.freedesktop.org/
8. Django REST framework. http://www.django-rest-framework.org/

Use of Web Components to Develop Interactive, Customizable and Multi-device Video Consumption Platforms

Mario Montagud[1,2], Fernando Boronat[1(✉)], Jordi Belda[1], and Dani Marfil[1]

[1] C/Paraninf, 1, 46730 Grao de Gandia, Valencia, Spain
`mamontor@upv.es, {fboronat,damarre}@dcom.upv.es,`
`jorbelva@epsg.upv.es`
[2] Science Park 123, 1098 XG Amsterdam, The Netherlands

Abstract. The recent and unceasing advances in Web technologies and components open the door to the development of a new wave of interactive, customizable and multi-device video consumption platforms. This chapter reviews various relevant Web technologies and components in the context of interactive media delivery and communication, and highlights a set of features and functionalities that can be provided by using these components. After that, two video consumption platforms that have been developed by combining these features and functionalities are presented. The first platform, called Wersync, enables the creation of different groups of geographically distributed users for consuming the same media content in a synchronized manner, while socially interacting via text and audiovisual chat channels. The second platform enables a dynamic customization and synchronization of subtitles in multi-screen scenarios. As a proof of evidence, links to demo videos showing the capabilities of both platforms are provided.

Keywords: IDES · Interactive media · HTML5 · Javascript · Online video · Subtitles customization · Synchronization · Web · WebRTC

1 Introduction

The World Wide Web (WWW) has progressively shifted from a document-based paradigm to a more distributed, interactive and collaborative form of media delivery and communication. A growing interest in integrating interactive media features into Web applications has recently led to the creation of various standard Web technologies (e.g., HTML5, Javascript, WebRTC…) and components that open the door to a new rich set of possibilities regarding media consumption and real-time multi-party communications, including different combinations of media content (e.g., audio, images, video, textual information…). These advancements also allow providing interaction, adaptation and customization features, as well as responsive and event-driven behavior, to the developed applications and services.

This chapter highlights the convenience and the possibilities of Web technologies and components for developing interactive, customizable and multi-device video consumption platforms. It introduces various relevant Web technologies and

© Springer International Publishing Switzerland 2016
M.J. Abásolo et al. (Eds.): jAUTI 2015/CTVDI 2015, CCIS 605, pp. 26–43, 2016.
DOI: 10.1007/978-3-319-38907-3_4

components and identifies their capabilities to provide different features and functionalities within the context of media delivery and communication. After that, as proofs of evidence, this chapter presents two video consumptions platforms that have been developed by combining the previously described features and functionalities. The first platform, called Wersync, enables the creation of different groups of geographically distributed users for consuming the same media content in a synchronized manner, while socially interacting. The social interaction, presence and privacy mechanisms provided by Wersync are also described. The second platform enables a dynamic customization, adaptation and synchronization of subtitles in multi-screen scenarios. The evaluation of both platforms is out of the scope of this chapter, but links to demo videos showing their capabilities are provided.

By exclusively relying on standard Web technologies and components, cross-network, cross-platform and cross-device (as well as cross-browser) support for the developed platforms can be ensured. Moreover, the use of Web components contributes to a better scalability, more efficient maintenance, as well as more ubiquitous, faster and easier deployment in heterogeneous over-the-top Internet environments.

It is important to note that despite of the increasing adoption of HTTP Adaptive Streaming (HAS) solutions for media delivery, such as Moving Picture Experts Group (MPEG) Dynamic Adaptive Streaming over HTTP (DASH), and their relevance within the context of this work, these solutions are not covered due to space limitation, but could be a perfect topic to be provided in a complementary work.

1.1 Web-Based Applications vs Native Applications

This sub-section provides a discussion about the suitability of using Web components instead of native (or platform-specific) components for developing media consumption platforms. This discussion is based on the analysis conducted in [1], by updating key aspects as well as adapting and extending it to our requirements.

Support. Native applications need to be specifically built for every target platform. Therefore, developers must take into account the number and types of target platforms in which the applications will be run. Moreover, it is not only a matter of the application environment (e.g., smartphone, tablet, PC, connected TV…) and brands (e.g., iPhone, Android, Windows…), but also of the platform version, as different versions can support different features or can perform differently. When an application needs to be supported by a new platform, it must be re-implemented using its native programming language, framework and characteristics.

In contrast, if standard components are used, Web applications can be deployed on any Web browser, regardless of the operating system and the type of client devices. Although slight differences regarding the support of specific features and the behavior between different platforms, browsers and even versions of the same browser may still exist, they are much smaller than in native applications. Moreover, these differences are progressively being overcome with the recent advances in web-based technologies. When the developed Web applications need to be supported by a new platform, much less effort is required, because the development of Web applications and services is based on the principle of *"build once, run anywhere"*.

Development. The development of native applications requires specific knowledge about each particular platform, due to the use of various underlying programming languages, associated frameworks, Software Development Kits (SDKs), style guidelines, etc. This generally implies an increase of costs, mainly because of the need for many developers, with different skills and specializations, and the availability of various development tools and frameworks.

In contrast, the development of Web applications mainly requires knowledge about the necessary web components (e.g., HTML, CSS and Javascript), thus avoiding the need to learn different programming languages and to become familiar with various development frameworks in order to provide cross-platform and cross-device support.

Although the use of native frameworks provides higher level of control and more possibilities than the use of Web components for the development of media applications, the differences are progressively disappearing since the inception and unceasing evolution of HTML5 and Javascript Application Programming Interfaces (APIs). For example, via Javascript APIs, it is possible to have control over capturing and rendering devices, USB devices, different sensors integrated with the client devices (e.g., accelerometer, GPS...), client's services (e.g., calendar, contacts...), etc. This enables the development of self-contained and complete applications by only using Web components. A current limitation of Web components is, however, the limited access and control over low-level information of the media streams being captured, delivered and consumed (e.g., buffering status, insertion and interpretation of timelines...).

Installation and Maintenance. The download and installation of native applications can depend on the application environment and on the device brand, but the current trend (mainly for companion devices) is to acquire them from *"app stores (or markets)"*. Publications and updates of applications on *app stores* may require the review and approval by store managers (e.g., for Apple devices). After the approval, applications can be downloaded and installed on the targeted devices under users' request.

In contrast, Web applications can be generally accessed through Web browsers, if they are (publicly) hosted on the Internet. Web applications do not need to be reviewed and approved by the managers of the (platform-specific) marketplaces, and they can be simply updated by modifying their code and resources on the server side. After that, the client devices can effectively receive and use the updated version of the application, without any further modification or installation.

It is worth to mention that hybrid solutions for Web applications are also possible. They consist of embedding Web applications into native applications (the so called *WebApps*) and then uploading them on platform-specific *app stores*.

Usability. Native applications have typically provided higher performance and a richer set of possibilities for designing more attractive and complete User Interfaces (UI) than Web applications. This results in a better usability of the developed applications and, in general, in a better user' perceived Quality of Experience (QoE). Although this statement can still be considered true, the differences are getting narrower, due to the recent and unceasing advances in Web components, especially within the context of media consumption applications.

Conclusion. Despite of the slight advantages of using native applications in terms of more complete support for specific platforms, performance and usability, the differences are not so significant, especially regarding the development of media consumption platforms, which is the scope of this work. On the other hand, the use of Web applications can contribute to reduce the costs in terms of development, maintenance and distribution (principle of *"build and update once, run anywhere"*). Moreover, it can guarantee a more flexible and successful cross-platform, cross-device and cross-browser support, and also cross-network support, as the Web traffic is not typically sensitive to firewall blocking policies and Network Address Translation (NAT) traversal issues. This last aspect contributes to a better ubiquity of the media applications and services to be deployed. All these considerations support our decision on choosing web-based technologies and components for developing the presented video consumption platforms.

1.2 Employed Web-Based Technological Components

In order to develop the targeted interactive and multi-screen video consumption platforms, several web-based technological components have been used[1]:

- HTML5 *video* element: it allows embedding full-fledged media players into webpages, selecting the specific path of the video files to be played out and their format (e.g., codec). In addition, the HTML5 *track* element is used to automatically retrieve and present subtitles and other timed text-based data.
- *Node.js*: it is an open-source, cross-platform runtime environment, written in Javascript, for server-side and networking web-based applications. *Node.js* provides a bidirectional event-driven communication model and a non-blocking I/O API for developing efficient and lightweight real-time distributed media applications. Moreover, *Node.js* contains a built-in module that allows to be used as a Web (and media) server, without the need of using additional servers, such as Apache or Internet Information Services (IIS) Server.
- *Socket.IO*: it is a lightweight Javascript library that enables real-time, bidirectional and event-driven communication between Web clients and a (*Node.js*) web server. *Socket.IO* primarily uses the WebSocket protocol (with polling as a fallback option), but it also provides many more features, including broadcasting to multiple sockets, storing data associated with each client, and asynchronous I/O. *Socket.IO* transparently handles the connection process and abstracts the underlying transport mechanisms (e.g., Websocket, AJAX...) in use. By using *Socket.IO*, different types of messages (with different data types) can be sent via a single communication channel.

---

[1] We would like to point out that these are the components we have used in/for our developments, but we do not state that all of them are mandatory. Moreover, other similar or extra components could also be employed for similar purposes.

- Clock Synchronization Mechanism: The availability of a coherent notion of time in a media session is a key requirement to achieve synchronized playback across devices. Accordingly, a virtual clock synchronization mechanism has been developed to recreate the functionalities of typical clock synchronization protocols (e.g., Network Time Protocol or NTP) in web-based scenarios.
- Social Media APIs: Most of the current Social Media platforms, such as Twitter and Facebook, provide web-based APIs and/or customized widgets. This allows, among other functionalities, embedding (almost all the features provided by) these platforms into webpages, customizing the platform offerings to the targeted requirements, logging in into applications or services by using the Social Media credentials, as well as providing tools for social media analytics (e.g., monitoring the users' satisfaction and preferences, implicitly acquiring relevant information from their activities and profiles…).
- Web Real-Time Communication (WebRTC): it is an open-source project (work in progress), currently under standardization within Internet Engineering Task Force (IETF) and World Wide Web Consortium (W3C). WebRTC enables real-time audio and video communications, as well as exchange of generic data (e.g., text chat, or files), between Web browsers via Javascript APIs, without the need of installing any software, plugin or third-party application.

By combining these components, the targeted interaction, customization, presence and synchronization features are provided in the developed video consumption platforms. Figure 1 provides a graphical overview of the involved entities (servers and clients) and components in the developed platforms, as well as of the communication models between them. Although the media, Web, synchronization and clock servers have been represented as independent entities for a better clarity, their functionalities can be implemented in a single (*Node.js*) server. In particular, this second option corresponds to our current implementations. The next sections describe the specific functionalities that have been implemented by using these components and the specific messages that are exchanged.

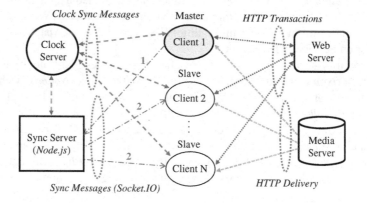

Fig. 1. Involved entities and exchange of messages in the developed platforms

1.3   Structure of the Chapter

This chapter is structured as follows. Section 2 describes the functionalities provided by the HTML5 *<video>* element to act as a self-sufficient and full-fledged media player, while Sect. 3 describes the capabilities of the HTLM5 *<track>* element to present subtitles in a synchronized manner with the associated audiovisual data. Section 4 presents the two components that have designed to achieve synchronized playback across devices in the developed platforms. Section 5 describes different web-based social interaction modalities that can be used in shared media experiences. Then, Sect. 6 presents the two platforms that have been developed, by using the Web components and functionalities described in the previous sections. Finally, Sect. 7 concludes the chapter and outlines some directions for future work.

2   HTML5 Video Player

The standard HTML5 *<video>* element allows embedding full-fledged media players into webpages. It takes a media file as in input (accepting WebM, OGG and MP4 container formats), which is specified via its *src* attribute. In order to provide multi-browser support, multiple *<source>* elements can be added inside a *<video>* element, each with a different *src* attribute linking to a different file with a particular encoding (and encapsulation) format. Accordingly, each client browser will select the first media file that it can properly decode and consume. The *<video>* element is self-sufficient to provide intra-media and inter-media synchronization (between audio and video), which means that it internally and transparently handles the aspects related to de-multiplexing, decoding, buffering and temporal presentation of media. Similarly, the *<audio>* element is used for playing audio files.

Playback control (e.g., play, pause, seeking, volume…) can be dynamically set by the users through the controls of the media player (by setting its *controls* attribute to *true*). Each media (*<audio>*, *<video>*) element can also have a *MediaController* object, which is used to coordinate a synchronized playback between multiple media elements. By default, a media element has no *MediaController*. An implicit *MediaController* can be assigned using a so called *mediagroup* content attribute. An explicit *MediaController* can be assigned directly using a so called *controller* IDL attribute of the media element. Media elements linked to a *MediaController* are slaved to it, which means that the play-back control (e.g., play, pause, seek…), rate and volume of each of the media elements slaved to a *MediaController* are shared. It also ensures that when any of the media elements stalls, the other media elements linked to the same *MediaController* are stopped at the same time.

3   Subtitles' Presentation and Customization

When using HTML5, subtitle files are linked to media files via the <track> element, which is a child of the (<audio> and <video>) element[2]. The <track> element accepts subtitle files in Web Video Text Tracks (WebVTT) format [2], which is the W3C standard for displaying timed text-based media. WebVTT provides a simple, extensible, and human-readable format on which text tracks can be built. A WebVTT subtitle file (with.*vtt* extension) is composed of various blocks or items, called *cues*. A *cue* basically contains an ID (optional), time settings (start and end time) relative to the media playback position, the text-based information and a blank line (end of the *cue*). The <track> element has several attributes: (i) *src*: the address of the WebVTT file; (ii) *srclang*: the language of the track; (iii) a user-readable and visible label (e.g., indicating the language of the subtitles); and (iv) *kind*: the type of track (subtitles, captions, descriptions, chapters or metadata). This element is capable of automatically handling the synchronization between the audiovisual content from the media element, and each *cue* of the subtitle file, by presenting it during the proper period interval, without the need of any additional scripting or software component. The presentation of each *cue* according to the media timeline is achieved by connecting to the *"cuechange"* event of the <track> element. Synchronization will be kept even when dynamic playback control changes are issued.

The <track> element can add different types of timed text-based media, which are specified by using its *kind* attribute. If the *kind* attribute is set to *"metadata"*, the information of the *cue* is not visible to the users, but its information can be retrieved and presented in other elements. By using this strategy, our platform enables the dynamic customization of the subtitles' format (e.g., color, font family, size, layout…), by using Cascading Style Sheets (CSS) style settings, as well as of the subtitles' position (e.g., drag and drop, replacement, even beyond the video window or the main screen…) to optimize their readability or the application's aesthetics. These style and position settings can be coordinated with the ones natively provided by the WebVTT format [2], and even extend them. The dynamic customization of subtitles will not affect to its synchronization with the audiovisual content.

4   Synchronization Across Devices

Apart from the synchronization between media elements within the same device (or more specifically within the same instance of a web browser), our targeted platforms require synchronization between media elements being played out on different devices, which can be located either at the same local environment (e.g., a multi-screen scenario) or at geographically distributed locations (e.g., in a Social TV scenario). To achieve this goal, two main components have been designed and developed. The first one is a virtual clock synchronization module, while the second one is an adaptive Inter-Device Synchronization (IDES) protocol. Both components are presented in the next sub-sections.

---

[2] It implies that no <track> element can be defined without the prior definition of an associated parent <video> (or <audio>) element.

4.1   Clock Synchronization Module

As previously mentioned, the availability of a global and coherent notion of time for all the involved entities in a shared media session is a key requirement to provide synchronized playback across devices.

Three alternatives could be employed to provide shared and common timelines for all the involved devices, all of them making use of clock synchronization mechanisms. The first option is to synchronize the clocks of the involved devices at the system-level (e.g., by using typical NTP clients). However, this may not be globally supported in multi-device and multi-platform ecosystems. A second option is to synchronize the clocks of the involved devices at the application-level, thus using a separate clock from the system clock for synchronization purposes. However, this option may involve the installation of additional modules (e.g., Javascript NTP clients) in the involved devices. Moreover, in the previous two options, it may be possible that the involved devices cannot access the same clock (e.g., NTP) server or that not all of them support the selected clock synchronization technology. Therefore, an ad-hoc virtual clock synchronization mechanism has been designed. It basically consists of having a reference clock server (e.g., co-located with the *Node.js* server) and adopting a *request-reply* protocol, based on periodically exchanging, via the *Socket.IO* channel (see Fig. 1), timestamped messages between the involved entities to estimate the Round-Trip-Time (RTT) delays and skews (i.e., offsets) between the local clock (provided by whatever technology) of each entity and the reference clock, in a similar way as NTP works. This allows time-aligning the clocks of the involved entities, even if they do not support the same technology for clock synchronization, and without the need for installing additional plugins or modules.

4.2   IDES Protocol

Apart from the virtual clock synchronization mechanism, an IDES protocol has been designed and implemented to achieve a globally synchronized playback in the shared session. It basically adopts an M/S Scheme [3], in which one device is considered the master and the rest are considered the slaves. Using M/S Scheme, the master device will periodically send control messages, called *IDES messages*, to the slave devices. The IDES messages will be sent via the *Socket.IO* channel, through the *Node.js* server (see Fig. 1). The transmission interval of the *IDES messages* can be configured (e.g., every 1 s) and can also be dynamically adjusted according to the number of active clients in the session to not overload the server and network resources.

Specifically, each device includes the following information into the *IDES messages*: (i) its current playout position: (ii) its current wall-clock (absolute) time; and (iii) the logical group to which it belongs. This last field allows an independent management of the synchronization process for different groups of clients in the same media session (e.g., when different groups of users are watching an online football match).

Upon receiving an *IDES message*, each client will calculate the asynchrony (i.e., the playout time difference) between its playout timing and the one reported in that *IDES message*. It is done by retrieving its current local playout position and comparing it with the one included in the *IDES message*. Moreover, the time difference between the reception and transmission instants of the *IDES message* is taken into account to compensate for the transit delay of the IDES message, thus achieving highly accurate synchronization. This is possible thanks to the developed clock synchronization mechanism. As a result, if the computed asynchrony exceeds an allowable (configurable) threshold, the client must adjust its playout timing to achieve IDES. The playout adjustments can be performed by two strategies: aggressive and smooth. First, aggressive strategies consist of performing simple skips and pauses, with a magnitude equal to the detected asynchrony. Second, the asynchrony can be eliminated by smoothly adjusting (i.e., either slowing down or fasting up) the playback rate during a specific time interval. This second strategy is much more convenient, because it provides higher synchronization accuracy and minimizes the occurrence of long-term playout interruptions, which can be annoying to users (poor QoE).

In geographically distributed scenarios (e.g., in Social TV), the IDES protocol can also adopt of a Synchronization Maestro Scheme (SMS) [3, 4]. Using SMS, all the clients in the shared session will send *IDES messages* to a centralized synchronization manager (which can be co-located with the *Node.js* server), which will process them and, if needed, will send back to the clients a new control message including the necessary playout adjustment to achieve IDES.

Apart from periodically reporting on media playout timing, the IDES protocol also allows distributing time-stamped navigation or VCR-like control commands (e.g., "play", "pause" or "jump to position"), also adding (relative and absolute) timestamps to achieve higher synchronization accuracy. This functionality enables interactive shared media sessions. For example, the video can be paused at all the clients to discuss about a specific scene, or it can be moved backward to jointly watch the repetition of a specific scene.

5   Web-Based Social Interaction Channels

In shared media experiences, like in Social TV, the involved geographically distributed users can socially interact and discuss about the media content being consumed through various modalities of communication channels, such as text chat tools and audio/video conferencing services (as well as combinations thereof). This section indicates these different modalities, including some variants for them (based on Web components), and briefly discusses some implications of their adoption in the targeted media consumption platforms.

5.1   Text-Based Chat Channels

This sub-section presents the two main options that can be chosen for including text-based chat channels in shared media experiences: the integration of Social Media platforms and the development of ad-hoc private chat channels. Besides, the pros and cons of their adoption are briefly discussed.

Integration of Social Media Platforms. The large popularity and mass adoption of Social Media is beyond doubt. Most of the current Social Media platforms, such as Twitter and Facebook, provide web-based APIs and/or customized widgets that allow their integration into websites or Web applications. For example, the APIs and a quite complete documentation about how to perform with the integration of Twitter and Facebook can be found at: https://dev.twitter.com (Twitter) and https://developers.facebook.com (Facebook).

From among all the rich set of functionalities that this integration can provide (mentioned in Sect. 1.2), we mainly focus on the use of these platforms as a text chat channel between the involved users in shared media experiences.

As a proof of evidence, different media sharing applications have integrated Social Media platforms, such as Twitter (e.g., in [4, 5]) and Facebook (e.g., in [5] and in [6]), by using their APIs.

Ad-hoc Private Text Chat Channels. An alternative to the integration of Social Media platforms is the development of an ad-hoc chat channel, fitting the targeted requirements of the application under development. For example, one option is to use the standard Extensible Messaging and Presence Protocol (XMPP), as in [7] and in [8], and another option is to use *Node.js* and *Socket.IO*, as in [4]. Both options provide good performance in terms of delays and allow the creation of several independent chat rooms in the same media session. Besides, both options, in coordination with the use of a clock synchronization mechanism (like the one presented in Sect. 4.1), allow the insertion of origination timestamps in each of the transmitted chat messages. This will enable their synchronization with the rest of chat messages and with the audiovisual content being consumed at the client side. A nice tutorial for the implementation of a chat channel using *Socket.IO* and *Node.js* can be found at: http://socket.io/get-started/chat/.

Discussion. The main advantages of the integration of Social Media platforms are: (i) the widespread adoption of these platforms, which allows interacting with a large amount of users who are consuming (or have consumed) the same media content as well as getting extra information about the media content; (ii) the possibility of retrieving and posting messages from/to official pages; (iii) the availability of multiple features provided by these platforms (e.g., the exchange of not only text messages, but also of images, photos and short clips, the availability of filtering mechanisms, such as hashtags, the availability of *like* and *share* functionalities...); (iv) the possibility of adding other sophisticated features (e.g., statistics, aggregation and filtering of information, event profiling and tracking, recommendations, sentiment mining...); etc. In contrast, the work in [9] identifies and discusses various limitations and constraints of using Social Media platforms, such as Facebook and Twitter, in media sharing applications. The most relevant ones are: (i) high end-to-end delays (i.e., delays between the instant at which a message is posted and the instant at which it is presented to the user); (ii) low flexibility for embedding and retrieving synchronization metadata (e.g., timelines); (iii) high dependence on third-party components and infrastructure; (iv) non-guaranteed scalability and availability (e.g., bounds in the traffic volume and/or rate per period of time); (v) need for filtering and refresh mechanisms, etc.

The end-to-end delay of messages from Social Networks can become a barrier in shared media experiences. It is because if the messages arrive too late, then they may be no longer relevant and can lead to confusion. This problem can be minimized when using ad-hoc chat tools because of the lower latency (i.e., better interactivity) and the higher flexibility for adding and interpreting timestamps (i.e., for achieving synchronization). The scalability and privacy issues that the use of "public" Social Networks may involve (with the exception of creating Facebook groups) can also be overcome by the creation of "private" chat rooms for each group when using ad-hoc chat tools, as previously mentioned. However, the adoption of ad-hoc chat tools has the drawback of having to add another chat tool, different from the ones customers are used to.

5.2   Audiovisual Chat Channels: WebRTC

A promising technology for proving web-based audiovisual communication channels is WebRTC. The W3C and the IETF are jointly working towards the specification and standardization of all the components involved in WebRTC technology. On the one hand, the RTCWeb group within the IETF is looking into issues like the identification of requirements and the definition of functionalities that must be supported by WebRTC. This group mainly focuses on networking related aspects, such as transport and control protocols, connection establishment and management, signaling mechanisms, topologies, selection of the most suitable encoders and decoders, and interoperability with other telecommunications systems. On the other hand, the WebRTC group within the W3C relies on the standardized components in IETF, and it is mainly concerned with the definition of Javascript APIs to allow the interaction between browsers and capturing and rendering devices, to negotiate and use certain parameters (e.g., encoders/decoders) and to set the appropriate protocols for communication. An overview of the WebRTC technology and of the associated standardization efforts within the W3C and IETF is given in [10, 11].

The most relevant WebRTC APIs include:

- *MediaStream* (a.k.a. *getUserMedia*): it allows the web browser to access the capturing devices (camera and microphone) and to capture media. It also provides the means to control where media content from the capturing devices can be consumed, and provides some control over these capturing devices.
- *RTCPeerConnection*: it handles stable and efficient communication of streaming data (e.g., audio/video calls) between Web browsers. The previous signaling process is not part of the WebRTC specification. Developers can choose the use of existing protocols, such as Session Initiation Protocol (SIP) or XMPP, or even develop an ad-hoc signaling mechanism to meet the targeted requirements.
- *RTCDataChannel*: it enables the exchange of arbitrary data (e.g., text chat, files…), with low latency and high throughput, between Web browsers in a peer-to-peer and bi-directional fashion.
- *getStats*: it allows retrieving a set of statistics about WebRTC sessions, both at the server side (e.g., frame rate, frame size, codec, packets/bytes sent, RTTs…) and at the client side (e.g., packet lost, jitter, packets/bytes/frames received and discarded,

frames rendered, playout delay…), as well as other types of statistics, such as the bandwidth usage, local/remote IP addresses and ports, type of connection, etc.

The support of the most relevant WebRTC components and APIs by different cross-platform browsers can be checked at: http://iswebrtcreadyyet.com/

The availability of audiovisual chat channels in shared media experiences is very relevant, as it may provide more natural, interactive, immersive and comfortable communications than the use of text chat channels.

As a proof of evidence, different media sharing platforms have integrated audiovisual communication services, such as a Voice over IP (VoIP) service (in [6] and in [7]) and a multi-party conferencing tool (in [8]), although this last one was more focused on the conferencing aspects than in the media sharing aspects.

6   Proof-of-Concept Implementations

This section briefly presents two proof-of-concept platforms that have been implemented by making use of the components described in the previous sections. Readers are referred to [4, 12] for a more complete documentation about these platforms and for consulting the benefits, advantages and novelties of these platforms compared to other existing ones of the same category.

6.1   Wersync

Shared media experiences between geographically distributed users are gaining momentum [3, 13]. Relevant examples are Social TV, synchronous e-learning, and multi-player online games. However, in order to successfully realize these experiences, proper platforms providing synchronization, social interaction and presence features, among others, are necessary. Due to this, we developed Wersync [4], an adaptive web-based platform for distributed media consumption and social interaction across remote users. Wersync allows the creation of independent groups of users, each of which being able to consume the same or different media content in a synchronized manner. When accessing to the platform, each user can choose between creating a new shared session (by also selecting the clip to be watched from an online video library) and joining an on-going one. Wersync provides two main social interaction mechanisms. First, it allows sharing the navigation control or VCR-like commands of the media player (i.e., play, pause and seek to) between all the users in a shared session. Second, it provides three social interaction channels, belonging to two different modalities: the first two ones are based on text-chat, while the third one is based on an audiovisual communication. In particular, the first one is based on integrating Twitter via its Javascript API. The drawback is, as previously mentioned, the interactivity limitations and the non-instantaneous refresh of the timeline. Moreover, the use of Twitter involves having a *"public"* chat room, even though some filtering mechanisms can be used, such as listening on a specific hashtag (e.g., *#Wersync*, or even adding the *session_id* as a suffix to the hashtag). The second one is an ad-hoc text chat tool, which has been developed by using *Socket.IO*. It provides much better performance in terms of delays than Twitter and allows the synchronization of the chat messages with the other media components being consumed in the shared session. Moreover, unlike Twitter, it also allows having private chat rooms for each shared session. The surveys and interviews we recently conducted with users (1015 participants) did not reveal significant differences between their preferences regarding the use of each one of the above types of text channels [13]. That is the reason we decided on integrating both of them in Wersync. Moreover, Twitter is used for another purpose, as explained next.

A third form of social interaction is currently under development. It consists of using WebRTC to provide a multi-party audiovisual chat channel between the participants in each shared session. It is expected that this modality of chat channel will provide a more comfortable, natural and realistic (face-to-face) interaction between users. Concretely, the results of the study in [13] indicate that 54 % of the participants prefer to use text chat channels, 11.1 % prefer to use voice chat channels and 34,8 % prefer to use audio-visual channels in Social TV-like scenarios.

Although the different chat channels have been added on the main screen, they could also have been implemented on the personal companion devices, by leveraging of the designed IDES protocol.

Wersync also provides three *"social presence"* mechanisms. The first one is an internal menu with drop-down lists, indicating the list of active sessions, their members and the media being consumed. This way, newcomers can check if they want to join any of the on-going sessions. The second one is an external presence mechanism, which consists of automatically posting a tweet every time a user creates or joins a session on Wersync (if he/she is logged in on Twitter and gives his/her consent for that). This tweet will include the appropriate information to univocally identify the shared session, including the user's nick in Wersync, the clip being consumed, hashtags (e.g., *#Wersync*, *#user_nick* and *#session_id*) and a URL to join the shared session (see Fig. 2). This announcement will allow external users to know about the activity of their Twitter contacts in Wersync, which will undoubtedly contribute to encourage their participation in on-going shared sessions. Additionally, the availability of audiovisual chat channels (implicitly) provides a third form of social presence.

Finally, Wersync provides two privacy mechanisms. First, despite of the Twitter notifications, the participation of new users in on-going shared sessions can be controlled. When each user requests to join a session, a message will be sent to the master/manager of that session, who can accept or reject that request. Second, the chat messages of the ad-hoc chat channel can be encrypted (if desired).

Mario Montagud @mario_montagud · 10 s
I'm watching "Sintel movie" (with nickname #Mario) on #Wersync in #Sintel_session: wersync.com/sintel_session @wersync

Fig. 2. Tweet informing about the activity of a user in Wersync

A general view of a Wersync client and of its functionalities can be seen in Fig. 3. Likewise, demo videos showing the capabilities of Wersync in shared media sessions can be watched at: goo.gl/6NjDRf.

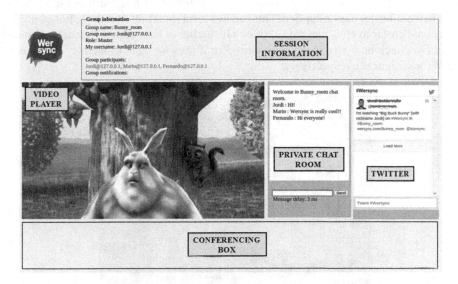

Fig. 3. Components and Structure of Wersync

Regarding its applicability, Wersync is not only targeted for entertainment purposes, such as Social TV, but also for other relevant use cases, such as e-learning and tele-work.

6.2 Subtitles' Synchronization and Customization Platform

Many application fields and benefits of subtitles can be emphasized. First, subtitles are very useful for users with audiovisual impairments. On the one hand, users with hearing impairments can (better) access to the audio information through subtitles. On the other hand, the customization of subtitles' format (e.g., size, font family, color…) can be very useful for people with visual impairments. Furthermore, subtitles are not only helpful for breaking down audiovisual barriers, but their applicability enters the realm of other forms of social integration, since they are powerful tools for consumers who do not (fully) understand the spoken language or accent (as they can select their native language for subtitles) or have comprehension difficulties. Subtitles are also very useful in educational environments, and are supportive tools for stimulating the cognitive processing, highlighting the relevance of specific pieces of media content, and for heightening the attention of consumers. Apart from the previous benefits, we believe that an adaptive and customizable presentation of subtitles is very beneficial to increase the comfort, engagement and, in general, the user's perceived QoE when consuming media content.

Due to these multiple benefits provided by subtitles, we have developed a web-based platform that enables a dynamic customization, adaptation and synchronization of subtitles in multi-screen scenarios (see Fig. 4). This platform enables the dynamic adaptation of subtitles' format (e.g., font family, size, color…) and position according to the users' preferences and/or needs. Likewise, the users can dynamically select the subtitles' language from the list of available ones through a drop drown list (see Fig. 5) and adjust the number of lines to be displayed. Moreover, a customized (positive or negative) delay offset to the subtitles can be applied. This can be useful in certain situations. For example, users could prefer to consume the subtitles a bit earlier or later than the associated audio content to check how words are pronounced or if they are able to identify the spoken words (or sentences), respectively.

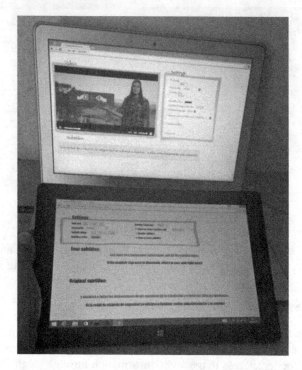

Fig. 4. Synchronization and Customization of Subtitles in Multi-Screen Scenarios

By using a companion device, each user can also personalize his/her subtitles consumption experience, enable the consumption of subtitles in two different languages (this can be very useful for language learning scenarios) and navigate between them, being able to set the position of the video by clicking on a specific subtitle line.

Synchronization between subtitles and the additional media content in the same device is achieved thanks to the native capabilities of HTML5 *<video>* and *<track>* elements. Synchronization across devices is achieved by using the designed clock synchronization mechanism and IDES protocol. The dynamic selection of the subtitles language is achieved by setting the proper values of the *src* and *srclang* attributes of the *<track>* element. The simultaneous consumption of the subtitles in two different languages when using a companion device is achieved by transmitting each *cue* of the subtitles presented on the main device via *Socket.IO*. The setting of delay offsets and presentation of various subtitles

Fig. 5. Subtitles' Language Selection

lines is achieved by loading and presenting the proper *cues* from the subtitle files, and, finally, the navigation between subtitles lines is achieved by interpreting the *start time* of the subtitle *cue* being clicked, and adjusting the playout position of the media player (*<video>* element) according to that value.

A distinctive and outstanding feature of our platform, compared to other existing ones (summarized in [13]), is that it is not only beneficial for the audience with hearing impairments, but also for the audience with visual impairments. It is because the dynamic and customizable settings of subtitles' format (e.g., family font, color, background color, size…) and the introduction of style effects, contribute to a better identification and comprehension for users with visual impairments. Furthermore, the dynamic positioning of subtitles in the main screen, but, specially, the (customizable) presentation of subtitles in each companion device allows for a much better readability, according to the users' needs and/or preferences, overcoming distance barriers and the presence of obstacles.

Our platform can be very useful in many use cases. First, it can contribute to a better social integration. On the one hand, it can be used by people with audiovisual impairments, who can adapt the subtitles' format according to their needs. On the other hand, apart from in domestic scenarios, it can be used in both public and private spaces where multi-culture people can happen to meet (e.g., touristic places, public transportations systems and stations…), allowing people from different countries the selection of their native language for subtitles by using their own companion device, as well as in crowded places (e.g., restaurants, museums…) where audio cannot be listened or its volume cannot be high. Third, it can be very beneficial for language therapy, literacy and learning purposes. Finally, it can contribute to a more pleasant, personalized and immersive experience (thus increasing the QoE) when consuming media content.

7   Conclusion and Future Work

This chapter has highlighted the convenience and possibilities of Web technologies and components for developing interactive, customizable and multi-device video consumption platforms. After reviewing various features and functionalities that can be provided by previously introduced Web components, two video consumptions platforms, developed by using these components, have been presented. The first platform, called Wersync, enables the creation of different groups of geographically distributed users for consuming the same media content in a synchronized manner, while socially interacting. The social interaction, presence and privacy mechanisms provided by Wersync have been also described. The second platform enables a dynamic customization, adaptation and synchronization of subtitles in multi-screen scenarios. By exclusively relying on standard web-based components, cross-network, cross-platform and cross-device (as well as cross-browser) support for the developed platforms can be ensured. Preliminary objective and subjective evaluations for both platforms have proved their satisfactory performance and usability, respectively. As a proof of evidence, links to demo videos showing the capabilities of both platforms have been provided.

As future work, several objectives have been planned. First, we want to improve the User Interface Design (UID) of the two developed platforms. Second, we want to extend their capabilities for also consuming and synchronizing live media, rather than solely stored media. Third, we want to more exhaustively evaluate the performance (Quality of Service or QoS) and the usability (QoE) of the developed platforms. Fourth, we want to adapt them to achieve a full compatibility with the HbbTV 2.0 standard [14]. Their fusion in a single platform is also a possibility we have in mind.

Acknowledgments. The work by Mario Montagud has been carried out during the tenure of an ERCIM 'Alain Bensoussan' Fellowship Programme. UPV work has been funded, partially, by the "Fondo Europeo de Desarrollo Regional (FEDER)" and the Spanish Ministry of Economy and Competitiveness, under its R&D&I Support Program, in project with reference TEC2013-45492-R.

References

1. Rodriguez, A., Talavera, G., Orero, P., Carrabina, J.: Subtitle synchronization across multiple screens and devices. Sensors **12**(7), 8710–8731 (2012)
2. Pfeiffer, S., Jägenstedt, P., Hickson, I. (eds.): WebVTT: The Web Video Text Tracks Format, W3C Community Group Draft (2015). http://dev.w3.org/html5/webvtt/
3. Montagud, M., Boronat, F., Stokking, H., van Brandenburg, R.: Inter-destination multimedia synchronization; schemes, use cases and standardization. Multimedia Syst. J. (Springer) **18**(6), 459–482 (2012)
4. Belda, J., Montagud, M., Boronat, F., Pastor, J.: Plataforma Web 2.0 para la Sincronización Distribuida de Contenidos Multimedia e Interacción Social. VI Congreso de TV Digital Interactiva – IV Jornadas Iberoamericanas de Aplicaciones y Usabilidad de la TVDi, Mallorca (Spain), October 2015
5. Dijkstra, S., et al.: STEER: Exploring the dynamic relationship between social information and networked media through experimentation. IEEE Comput. Soc. Spec. Techn. Commun. Soc. Netw. (STCSN) E-Lett., **3**(2), December 2015
6. Wijnants, M., Dierckx, J., Quax P., Lamotte, W.: Synchronous MediaSharing: social and communal media consumption for geographically dispersed users. In: MMSys 2012, North Carolina, USA, February 2012
7. Geerts, D., et al.: Are we in sync?: synchronization requirements for watching online video together. In: ACM CHI 2011, Vancouver, Canada, May 2011

8. Jansen, J., Cesar, P., Bulterman, D.C.A.: Multimedia document synchronization in a distributed social context. In: ACM DocEng 2013, Florence, Italy, September 2013
9. Wijnants, M., Quax, P., Lamotte, W.: Cost-effective web-based media synchronization schemes for real-time distributed groupware. In: WEBIST 2013, Auchen, Germany, May 2013
10. Loreto, S., Romano, S.P.: Real-time communications in the web: issues, achievements, and ongoing standardization efforts. IEEE Internet Comput. **16**(5), 68–73 (2012)
11. Jennings, C., Hardie, T., Westerlund, M.: Real-time communications for the web. IEEE Commun. Mag. **51**(4), 20–26 (2013)
12. Parcheta, Z., Montagud, M., Belda, J., Boronat, F.: Personalización y Sincronización de Subtítulos en Escenarios Multi-Pantalla. VI Congreso de TV Digital Interactiva – IV Jornadas Iberoamericanas de Aplicaciones y Usabilidad de la TVDi, Mallorca, Spain, October 2015
13. Boronat, F., Montagud, M., Martínez, M., Marfil, D.: Preferencias, necesidades y expectativas de los usuarios españoles en escenarios multimedia híbridos broadcast/broadband. VI Congreso de TV Digital Interactiva – IV Jornadas Iberoamericanas de Aplicaciones y Usabilidad de la TVDi, Mallorca, Spain, October 2015
14. HbbTV Hybrid Broadcast Broadband TV version 2, ETSI TS 102 796 v1.3.1, October 2015. hbbtv.org

An Augmented Reality and 360-degree Video System to Access Audiovisual Content through Mobile Devices for Touristic Applications

Antoni Bibiloni[2], Silvia Ramis[1(✉)], Antoni Oliver[2], and Francisco J. Perales[1]

[1] Unidad de Gráficos y Visión por Ordenador e IA, Palma de Mallorca, Islas Baleares, Spain
{silvia.ramis,paco.perales}@uib.es
[2] Laboratorio de Tecnologías Multimedia (LTIM), Departamento de Matemáticas e Informática,
Universitat de les Illes Balears (UIB), Palma de Mallorca, Islas Baleares, Spain
{toni.bibiloni,antoni.oliver}@uib.es

Abstract. In the recent years, consumption and usage of multimedia content has shifted to handheld devices, especially with the introduction of second screen applications. In this paper we address the situation of delivering multimedia information to users using modern and novel techniques to attract their attention in environments like fairs, parties or showrooms in an entertaining and educative way. Two different approaches are presented: an Augmented Reality application on mobile devices and a 360-degree video player remotely controlled by a handheld device. Both ideas focus on the use of mobile devices, as they have become a powerful tool always worn by its owners.

Keywords: Augmented reality mobile · 360-degree video · Omnidirectional video · Mobile applications · HTML5 web apps

1 Introduction

Nowadays, trying to deliver a piece information to an audience may be a difficult task, given that the attention of this audience may be in other targets that interest them more. For this reason, we have made an effort to try to get the users' attention with modern and novel techniques to access multimedia content with their own mobile devices.

We focused on the following scenario: given a vertical surface, we wanted to attract the visitors' attention to the media displayed on it. More specifically, our target was a touristic promotion faire, showcasing pictures and videos of the Balearic Islands. Of course, the system proposed in this work can be generalized to other touristic areas or industries related with tourism.

To address this problem, we introduce two different approaches: an Augmented Reality system on mobile devices, used to play multimedia content in the handheld, based on the pictures placed around that vertical surface; and a multi-user application, used to display omnidirectional video on TV screens, controlled by the movement of the users' handheld device. The main contribution of this work is to improve solutions based in new emerging technologies and translate this paradigm of natural interaction

© Springer International Publishing Switzerland 2016
M.J. Abásolo et al. (Eds.): jAUTI 2015/CTVDI 2015, CCIS 605, pp. 44–58, 2016.
DOI: 10.1007/978-3-319-38907-3_5

to low cost and portable devices in real and natural scenarios (fairs, parties, showrooms, etc.). The methodology proposed is based on standards tools for developing AR & 360° applications so as to guarantee the portability of the results to any platform.

This paper is structured in five sections. Following this one, the state of the art is presented to introduce the reader in the current situation of Augmented Reality and 360-degree video techniques and applications. In the third section, the two proposed solutions are introduced and explained in detail. Finally, in the fourth section the obtained results are shown. This paper ends with some conclusions and future improvement ideas.

2   State of the Art

The beginnings of augmented reality date back to 1960, when Sutherland [29] develops the first VR-helmet to display three-dimensional graphics. However, the term Augmented Reality was not created until 1992 by Caudell et al. [30]. In [14] the use of an HMD (Head Mounted Display) is described to "increase" the visual field of the user with information needed to perform the current task. In the late 90s, Kato et al. [31] develop the first software for the realization of Augmented Reality applications (ARToolkit). But it was not widely used until the emergence of smartphones, when this technology is driven for the development of Augmented Reality applications in various sectors, such as tourism or medicine, among many others, providing a better and more intuitive user experience through new interfaces and content.

Specifically, touristic activity is a significant economic base for many countries. Tourists are increasingly looking for applications and tools to facilitate and improve their travelling experience [18]. The motivation for most tourists is to explore the sights, history and locations of the visited place. One of the first places benefited by the augmented reality was the virtual reconstruction of the ancient temple of Olympia in Greece, where researchers developed the ARCHEOGUIDE system [19]. Recently, works like Yovcheva et al. [21] present an overview of the applications of RA in current smartphones related to tourism. The work of Marques [20] develops an application using geolocation to link historical and cultural information of the "Camino de Santiago". In [22] an application based on augmented reality is presented, which shows a video of a route through the city of "Santa Cruz de Tenerife" where all historical buildings are displayed with 3D animations. Kourouthanassis et al. [24] present a travel guide of the island of Corfu (Greece) for Android platforms, which enables the users to create a profile, allowing them to rate the places they have visited and recommend them to others. This way one can classify users depending on their profile and thus provide personalized content in the application. Chen [25] presents an application for the tourists interested in the history of Oslo (Norway), featuring two modules: a map to navigate and view the various points of interest, and an Augmented Reality module, showing an old picture of the place where the camera points, as well as access to historical information. Lashkari et al. [26] present a tourist catalog that uses augmented reality to show 3D objects on a simple map created with markers. Mohammed-Amin et al. [27] present a work based on the story of Arabella (Iraq), depicting a village with numerous and important archaeological layers. The application restores the damaged buildings, displaying them in 3D while one walks through the building structure. The users can access information about the place they see or locate their position on the in-app map. Mata et al. [28] present an augmented reality navigation interface that suggests places to visit in Mexico City. This system generates routes based on user behavior through the decision tree algorithm and the Bayes classifier. Other applications such as Flax et al. [23] encourage people to visit and explore the natural environment, such as a mountain, telling them its hidden story. This project also explores how augmented reality games can be used to provide an attractive tourist experience.

In recent years, various applications of augmented reality for mobile devices have been developed for the tourism industry, from 3D reconstructions based on geolocation and /or markers, even AR games that enhance learning and user experience.

On the other hand, the public perceives 360° video as a novel medium to live an immersive experience. Bleumers et al. [1] introduce many user expectations of omni-directional video. 360 degree immersive video consumption is seeing its popularity grow these last years, partly because popular video solutions, as YouTube [2] or Facebook [3] are beginning to offer immersive 360° video upload and visualization as a part of their services. Playback of 360 degree equirectangular video is supported in HTML5 browsers thanks to the powerful additions of WebGL [4], introduced in 2011. Android and iOS apps have also spread thanks to native support for video textures. Kolor Eyes [5], a solution for multiple platforms, is widely used by professionals. The user interaction with these applications can be in two different ways: either dragging with a pointing device (such as a mouse or a touch screen), or using sensors (typically from a specially made device, such as Oculus Rift [6], or using a smartphone, like in Google Cardboard [7]). From the previous works presented in this section, we can conclude that the new technologies based on AR and omnidirectional video are very interesting, presenting an area with a large growth and with many commercial applications, in particularly in the tourism industry.

3   Methodology

In this section, the development of the two proposed solutions is described: first, the Augmented Reality mobile application and then the Interactive Omnidirectional video player. These two solutions are complementary and show different ways to visualize augmentative and/or immersive scenarios.

3.1   Augmented Reality Mobile Application

In order to carry out a mobile AR system, it is necessary to use a device (in this case smartphones or tablets) that collects the reality, and software to detect, recognize and track a viewpoint. There are several methods to solve the problem of viewpoint tracking, such as using GPS location, or artificial vision (markers, hands, faces, etc.). The virtual objects are placed in calculated positions and displayed on the real world.

Available Tools for Augmented Reality. Since the creation of the first AR library (ARToolKit), there have been similar alternatives. Some of the options explored are cited (Table 1). For more details about Augmented Reality SDK's see [32].

Table 1. Tools for augmented reality

AR libraries	Observations
HandyAR	A library that allows to detect and track the hand to use it as a reference standard in augmented reality applications
AndAR	A Java library to create Augmented Reality applications for Android based on markers. It allows to find a marker on the scene and calculate the transformation matrix to render a virtual object in the location and orientation of the marker. Currently it does not support OpenGL 2.0
Atomic Web Authoring Tool	A tool that allows to create Augmented Reality applications and exportat them to any website
Atomic Authoring Tool	A tool that allows to create Augmented Reality applications, intended to be used by non-developers
ARToolKit	A library based on markers and tracking of natural features for iOS and Android. It is also supported by Unity, although it requires a Unity Pro license (paid version)
Wikitude SDK	A non-free library, with a trial version that contains a watermark, supported by iOS, Blackberry and Android. It allows to use the GPS system to geolocate the user
Vuforia (Qualcomm AR SDK)	A library that allows to create Augmented Reality applications for mobile devices, both iOS and Android. It enables to detect and track reference images or markers using detection features. It provides Unity support and has a free version

Given the nature of this work, which requires to support both Android and iOS devices, the Vuforia library is chosen because it presents an advanced image recognition engine, and is directly integrated with Unity. Unity is a powerful engine to develop games in 2D and 3D, offering total control to create and deploy content on any platform such as Linux, iOS, Android, Web, Mac, Windows, Windows Phone 8, among others. There are two versions of Unity: Unity Pro (the paid version) and the free version with which this work was done. In spite of having limitations with the free version, the functionality of the proposed application is complete.

Application Design. The application is designed to discover different places of the Balearic Islands in an easy and interactive way through mobile devices or tablets. With this system the user can interact, for example, with a catalogue of images where each image (target) is a photograph of a representative location of the Balearic Islands. Each target gives access to a different digital content, in this case the most representative locations of the Balearic Islands. The user can interact with the application through their mobile or tablet and recognize several targets simultaneously, select the desired target (place of the islands that interests him or her), play the related video, change the target, etc.

The images captured by the camera of the user's device are treated and compared with a database, where the targets were previously stored. If one of the targets is displayed on the scene captured by the camera, the video associated to the target will load. Each video has two possible states:

- Loading video. A loading icon is displayed on the video. It means that the application is connecting to the server where videos are stored.
- Play video. When the loading icon disappears, the video is ready to play.

For the performance of this application, two basic elements of Vuforia's Prefabs (ARCamera and Image Target) are used. The Prefabs are displayed in the Unity project, once the Vuforia library is imported. The trackable elements are shown in the Prefabs and treated in the tracker block (Vuforia). The most important Prefab element is the ARCamera, which is the point of view of the camera.

Besides these two Vuforia elements, two more elements are needed: the SceneManager, that handles various scenes of the application and the Directional light, used to illuminate scenes and objects.

Therefore, the first option is often to create an application using layers and buttons. In this option, the user can select the desired target by tapping on it to access its related content. Two buttons appear at the bottom of the screen: the *play icon* plays the digital content in full screen and the *google icon* places the target on Google Maps. To return to the Android application, the physical return button can be pressed. In Fig. 1 the interaction scheme is shown.

Since the emergence of smartphones, gestures have been introduced into our daily lives to interact with these devices. Therefore, we study the possibility of creating an application based on gestures and subsequently evaluate its usability. When creating an application, issues such as usability and design are raised. In order to develop an application as simple as possible and easy to understand, we used the gestures proposed in [33].

An example of this work is given in Fig. 2. The application consists of three simple gestures, which are easy to remember and can be used at any time. The "expand" gesture is known worldwide, used to display the video in full screen. The "one touch" gesture is used to select the video and play it over the image. If the user want to pause it, he or she can use the same gesture on the playback. Finally, the "two touches" gesture has been chosen to place the selected image on Google Maps.

After testing both solutions for the AR application, the experts concluded that the gestures are a more attractive and simple solution for the users.

3.2   Interactive Omnidirectional Video Player

A multi-user media controller and player for 360 degree video content were designed for the specific use case of an event demonstration, such as a fair. The video content is be played in a television, controlled by a PC and directed by the actions of the many users in their smartphones, one at a time.

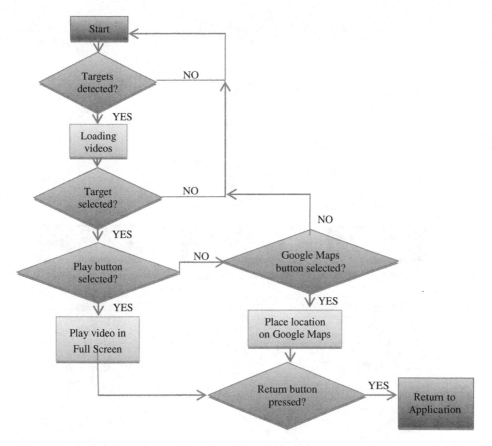

Fig. 1. Operating diagram of the application in mode of buttons

The multimedia catalogue mainly consists of 360 degree video content, but also regular video content can be played. These contents have additional information related to them, optionally temporarily placed.

Specific Requirements. In the midst of an event, users do not want to download a smartphone app only to play for some minutes. For this reason, a HTML5 web app, which does not require a download, is preferred.

Internet connections in many events may be faulty or insufficient for media streaming purposes, so the servers need to be accessed by using a local Wi-Fi network. Moreover, it can be impossible to download an app from Play Store or App Store, strengthening the above decision.

A queuing system had been implemented: while a user controls the video playback, the other users in the queue receive information about what is being played.

It is desired that many TVs can display different videos at the same time, independently from each other, so users would queue for controlling a specific TV.

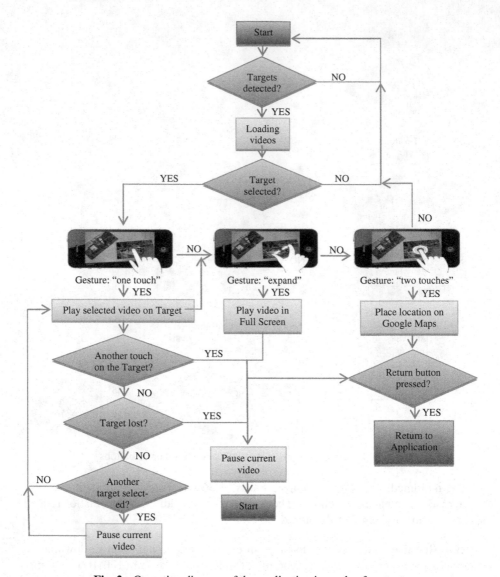

Fig. 2. Operating diagram of the application in mode of gestures

Proposed Solution. Three applications are designed:

- A mobile app, in order to control the playback of the video on a TV app and receive additional information related to it. This will run on Chrome for Android and Safari for iOS smartphones.
- A TV app, so as to play the specified video content according to the users' command. This will run on Chrome for a Windows desktop.

- A catalogue managing app, so as to add, edit and remove audiovisual content and their associated information from the catalogue. This will run on a web browser for desktop.

Two servers are also designed to assist these applications:

- The Master Server is a web server which hosts the previous web applications and also a Web Socket server which enables their communication with each other.
- The TV Servers are web servers which only host the multimedia resources used by a TV, in order to save bandwidth.

The Master Server is designed to also carry the functionality of a TV Server.

Data Model. The main entity of this project are the audiovisual resources, which can be of two types: `video` or `video360`. Other attributes are its title, the path of the mp4 file that contains the video, a thumbnail, a filtering property and whether or not this video should be auto-played when the TV is idle.

A description, in HTML, is attached to every resource, as well as the path to a background image to be displayed along it.

Finally, a video can have any number of temporarily placed fragments of information, called *pushes*, described by their title, time of appearance since the start of the video (in seconds), textual information in HTML and the path to a picture to be displayed as a background.

This data is stored in a XML file, and can be edited with the aid of the catalogue managing app. Paths inside this file should be relative to a folder containing all the audiovisual resources used by the project, which is replicated in every computer that is used as a TV Server.

Architecture. The hardware elements considered are the following:

- A Wi-Fi router.
- A server and a TV for each display.
- Personal mobile devices.

In Fig. 3 these items are displayed, as well as their relations: solid connections represent wired connections (such as HDMI or Ethernet); pointed connections mean logical relations (U_1 and U_2 are connected to the contents displayed on TV_1); dashed connections represent orders between the Interaction Server (inside S_1 in Fig. 3) and its clients, which can be the users' smartphones or the TV Servers.

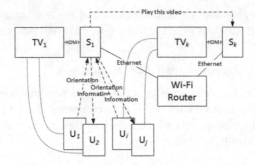

Fig. 3. Architecture of the proposed solution

Communication Protocol. The two clients establish a Web Socket [8] connection with the Interaction Server on startup. Following the users' actions, a series of commands are submitted from an application to the other through the Interaction Server, as can be seen in Fig. 4.

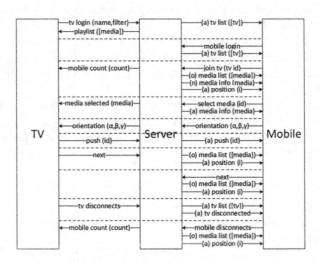

Fig. 4. Communication diagram. (a) denotes a message sent to all mobiles, (o) to only the TV owner and (n) to the non-owners of that TV.

From a TV perspective, the first command issued is `tv login`, accompanied by its name and filter property. With that information, the server appends it to the TV list, notifying already connected mobile devices with a `tv list` command, and selects the media list that will be played on this TV with the `playlist` command.

When a Mobile application connects to the Interaction server, it sends the `login` command, answered by `tv list` to build the TV list on the mobile.

When the user selects a TV from the list, the `join tv` command is issued, unless there is only a single TV in the list: in this case the command is sent automatically. The response from the Interaction server depends on whether the user becomes the owner of the TV or not. If he or she becomes the owner, the media list command is issued; otherwise, if a media has been selected, the media info command is sent. Regardless of that, the position command is issued with their current position in the queue.

In the moment in which the TV owner selects a media to play, the select media command is sent to the server, which sends the media selected command to the TV application, so as to begin its playback attaching its media path and pushes, and the media info command to the mobiles connected to that TV.

Whenever an orientation change occurs in the TV owner's Mobile application, the orientation message is sent to the server and redirected to the proper TV application to adjust the view of the 360-degree video.

The TV application sends a push command when a new piece of information is available, redirected to all the users connected to that TV.

When a video ends, the TV application sends the next command, making the server to shift the users' position in the queue. The new owner is given the media list with a media list message and all the connected users receive their updated position via a position command.

When a Mobile application is minimized, it sends the next command to the server, leaving its position in the queue. If necessary, a new owner is designated and the media list is sent. All the users get their position updated. A similar behavior is performed when a mobile application gets disconnected.

Finally, when a TV disconnects, all the users get the updated tv list and the mobiles connected to that TV get the tv disconnected message, so as to prompt the user to select another TV.

Developed System. Once the system was designed, we implemented the various servers and applications.

First, a public Wi-Fi network is set up on a router. The servers are connected to it through Ethernet. This way the mobiles can reach the Mobile application on the Interaction server.

So as not to type the IP address of the Interaction server to access the Mobile application, a DNS server is run within the computer that runs the Interaction server. Stackia's DNS Agent [9] is used for this reason, pointing an arbitrary domain name or pattern to the IP of the server. Finally, this server needs to be specified as the primary DNS server for the network in the settings of the router.

The Interaction Server is written in Node.js [10] and it fulfills the following tasks:

1. Read the configuration file (data.xml) and set up the data structures as defined previously, thanks to the Xml2js library [11].
2. As an HTTP Server, serves the TV, Mobile and the catalogue managing web applications, using the Express library [12]. It also serves the multimedia resources played in a TV.
3. As a Web Socket Server, listens for the events described in Communication protocol, thanks to the Socket.io library [13].

In order to enable the TV servers to serve the multimedia content from the local host, CORS must be enabled in the sent HTTP headers.

The TV server is a simplification of the Interaction server, serving only the multimedia resources that will be played from the TV application running in the local host.

The TV application features a loop of selected videos while idle and plays a specific multimedia resource on demand. It is implemented in HTML5 and is intended to be run full screen on a browser.

On startup, the application connects to the Interaction server and the user is prompted to enter a name for the TV and establish its filtering property, used to display a selection of the multimedia resources available. After that, the playback of the idle loop starts.

When a user connects to this TV, it becomes its owner if he or she is the only user connected to it and may choose a video to play on the TV. If it is a regular video, an HTML5 <video> element is used; but when a 360° video is selected, it must be rendered adequately. To do so, the video is also played in a–now hidden– <video> element, used as a texture on a 3D sphere, viewed from inside by the camera. This 3D work is done thanks to the Three.js library [14]. When the user's mobile orientation is received, the orientation of the camera is adjusted accordingly, in a 6:1 ratio (a 360° loop in the video is achieved with only a 60° swift in the mobile device, so as to permit the user to read the information in the screen).

The TV application keeps track of the play time of the video and notifies the connected users when a new piece of information has to be delivered.

Finally, when the video ends, the idle loop starts again and the TV is under control of the next user in the queue, if any. To start a TV application, the organizer has to browse to http://domain/tv and enter its name and filter properties.

On the user side, the Mobile application consists of a remote control application, permitting the user to select a TV to connect to and select a video to play on it. It also enables the user to orient a 360° video as well as to receive pieces of information related to a multimedia resource. It is also an HTML5 application, to be used only on smartphones. On startup, the application is connected to the Interaction server and receives a list of currently logged in TV applications (Fig. 5), so as the user can choose one of them. After that, or if it were a single TV logged in, the user queues for that TV and, in the case he or she becomes its owner, its media list is shown.

Fig. 5. Mobile application interface

The owner of a TV can choose what video should be played next and, if that video is a 360° content, orient it thanks to the user's device orientation. This is achieved thanks to the DeviceOrientation event [15], and more specifically, its alpha property, which describes the rotation of the device through its z-axis, perpendicular to the screen. A user is not the owner of a TV indefinitely: a next command will be issued when the selected video ends, the socket connection closes, the application is minimized (thanks to the onVisibilityChange event [16]) or the owner takes more than 30 s to choose a video to play.

Whether a user is the owner of the TV or not, they will receive pieces of information as they are sent by the Interaction server. These will usually be accompanied with a picture.

Three buttons are shown in the toolbar: the search button, to find a specific media resource; the TV list button, to go back to the TV selection screen; and the media list button, to select another video resource.

The application is styled with the Material Design Lite CSS library [17], to make it look as a Material application.

Users should connect to the special Wi-Fi network and then navigate to http:// domain/ to open the Mobile application.

Finally, the catalogue managing application is a web form that permits the user to edit the information used by the system, described in Data model. It features two buttons: one to reload the data used currently by the server and another one to overwrite it. After that, the server must be rebooted.

To edit the information used by the system, one should navigate to http://domain/ data.

From the two approaches presented in this section, we can conclude that immersive and augmented reality solutions are valid to increase the user participation in the multimedia applications. In our case, these solutions work independently, although new paradigms that propose hybrid virtual reality/video systems can be explored.

4   Results

The results of the work presented in this paper are two separate approaches to attract the users' attention in a touristic promotion faire with modern technologies. Both applications (Fig. 6) underwent a preliminary stage of testing. In particular, the AR system has been tested with 32 multimedia videos, which have been stored in a server and have been associated to an image (Target). These targets have been stored in a local database on the mobile device, because Vuforia library allows creating a free database that supports until 100 targets. Also, it has been proved on Android and iOS, in particular on an iPad and a mid-range Android mobile; while the 360-degree video player behave successfully on both Android and iOS devices, being able the entire set of 20 omnidirectional video files on the TV application, which was always run on the Chrome web explorer on a Windows machine.

Fig. 6. On the left, AR Mobile application. On the right, Omnidirectional Video player.

The two systems were introduced to a group of three experts, professionals of the touristic sector, who tested both solutions focusing on the following key aspects: ease of use, attractiveness, efficiency, functionality and specific restraints in a faire setup. After that, they evidenced the advantages and disadvantages of both systems:

1. On one hand, the AR Mobile application was praised to be very simple and appealing, although its need of a stable Internet connection and having to download an application from App Store or Google Play challenged the viability of this solution for this kind of events.
2. On the other hand, even though the Omnidirectional Video player was designed to overcome these connection issues, the experts believed that it was more complex and would be difficult to understand by the users without a proper explanation.

In the end, the experts exposed that a complement of the two solutions would be ideal and chose to make a proof of concept of the Omnidirectional Video player in FITUR[1], where it would be used with the aid of the staff.

5   Conclusion

The system proposed shows a new way to visualize and interact with multimedia products in real environments. We would like to promote new immersive and augmented systems for the end user in order to attract their attention to touristic products. Both systems are complementary and have friendly interfaces and portable and multiplatform devices and operating systems.

The two solutions developed above were tested by tourism professionals to prove that it can be really used to attract the users' attention towards the multimedia information these professionals wanted to deliver to their potential customers.

From a technological perspective, the AR mobile application was proven to be very simple and attractive, although it needs a stable Internet connection to connect to the server and play the multimedia content. On the other side, the Omnidirectional video player was perceived as a more complicated application, with excessive mess with queues, although it adequately met the strict requirements.

---

[1] Feria Internacional del Turismo, http://www.ifema.es/fitur_01/.

After having developed and used both solutions, it has been noticed that the combination of both solutions is possible to offer a better solution, and we would like to work on this research line as future work, using the simpler concept of the AR mobile application and the constraints of a local HTML5 application, like the Omnidirectional video player, and conduct a proper usability test on the final product.

References

1. Bleumers, L., Van den Broeck, W., Lievens, B., Pierson, J.: Seeing the bigger picture: a user perspective on 360° TV. In: Proceedings of the 10th European Conference on Interactive TV and Video, EuroiTV 2012, pp. 115–124. ACM (2012)
2. YouTube Creator Blog: A new way to see and share your world with 360-degree video [website] (2015). http://youtubecreator.blogspot.com.es/2015/03/a-new-way-to-see-and-share-your-world.html. Accessed 1 Dec 2015
3. Facebook Media: 360 video [website] (2015). https://www.facebook.com/facebookmedia/get-started/360-video. Accessed 1 Dec 2015
4. Khronos Group: WebGL - OpenGL ES 2.0 for the Web [website] (2015). https://www.khronos.org/webgl/. Accessed 1 Dec 2015
5. Kolor: Kolor Eyes [website] (2015). http://www.kolor.com/kolor-eyes/. Accessed 1 Dec 2015
6. Oculus VR, LLC: Oculus [website] (2015). https://www.oculus.com/. Accessed 1 Dec 2015
7. Google: Google Cardboard [website] (2015). https://www.google.com/get/cardboard/. Accessed 1 Dec 2015
8. Fette, I., Melnikov, A.: The WebSocket protocol. In: IETF Internet Draft (2011). https://tools.ietf.org/html/rfc6455
9. Stackia: DNSAgent: a powerful "hosts" replacement [website] (2015). https://github.com/stackia/DNSAgent. Accessed 1 Dec 2015
10. Node.js Foundation: "Node.js" [website] (2015). https://nodejs.org. Accessed 1 Dec 2015
11. Leonidas-from-XIV: node-xml2js: XML to JavaScript object converter [website] (2015). https://github.com/Leonidas-from-XIV/node-xml2js. Accessed 1 Dec 2015
12. StrongLoop: Express - Node.js web application framework [website] (2015). http://expressjs.com/. Accessed 1 Dec 2015
13. Socket.IO Contributors: Socket.IO [website] (2015). http://socket.io/. Accessed 1 Dec 2015
14. Three.js: three.js - Javascript 3D library [website] (2015). http://threejs.org/. Accessed 1 Dec 2015
15. W3C: DeviceOrientation event specification. In: W3C Working Draft (2011). https://www.w3.org/TR/orientation-event/
16. W3C: Page Visibility (Second Edition). W3C Recommendation (2013). https://www.w3.org/TR/page-visibility/
17. Google: Material Design Lite [website] (2015). http://www.getmdl.io/. Accessed 1 Dec 2015
18. Park, D., Nam, T.J., Shi, C.K.: Designing an immersive tour experience system for cultural tour sites. In Proceedings of CHI'06. Extended Abstracts, pp. 1193–1198 (2006)
19. Gleue, T., Dähne, P.: Design and implementation of a mobile device for outdoor augmented reality in the archeoguide project. In: Proceedings of the 2001 conference on Virtual reality, archeology, and cultural heritage, pp. 161–168 (2001)
20. Marques, M.N.: S.I.G. E Realidade aumentada em turismo – Guia interactivo do Caminho Português de Santiago em Barcelos. Tesis. Universidad de Santiago de Compostela (2014)

21. Yovcheva, Z., Buhalis, D., Gatzidis, C.: Overview of smartphone augmented reality applications for tourism. e-Rev. Tour. Res. (eRTR) **10**(2), 63–66 (2012)
22. Fino, E.R., Martín-Gutiérrez, J., Fernández, M.D.M., Davara, E.A.: Interactive tourist guide: connecting web 2.0, augmented reality and QR codes. Procedia Comput. Sci. **25**, 338–344 (2013)
23. Linaza, M.T., Gutierrez, A., García, A.: Pervasive augmented reality games to experience tourism destinations. In: Xiang, Z., Tussyadiah, I. (eds.) Information and Communication Technologies in Tourism, pp. 497–509. Springer, New York (2014)
24. Kourouthanassis, P., Boletsis, C., Bardaki, C., Chasanidou, D.: Tourists responses to mobile augmented reality travel guides: the role of emotions on adoption behavior. Pervasive Mob. Comput. **18**, 71–87 (2014)
25. Chen, W.: Historical oslo on a handheld device – a mobile augmented reality application. Procedia Comput. Sci. **35**(1877), 979–985 (2014)
26. Lashkari, A.H., Parhizkar, B., Mohamedali, M.A.: Augmented reality tourist catalogue using mobile technology. In: Second International Conference on Computer Research and Development, no. Fig. 1, pp. 121–125 (2010)
27. Mohammed-Amin, R.K., Levy, R.M., Boyd, J.E.: Mobile augmented reality for interpretation of archaeological sites, PATCH 2012, Nara, Japan, 2 November 2012
28. Mata, F., Claramunt, C.: A social navigation guide using augmented reality. In: Proceedings of 22nd ACM SIGSPATIAL Internetional Conference on Advanced Geographic Information Systems - SIGSPATIAL 2014, pp. 541–544 (2014)
29. Sutherland, I.E.: A head-mounted three- dimensional display. In: AFWS Conference Proceedings 1968 Fall Joint Computer Conference, vol. 33, pp. 757–764 (1968)
30. Caudell, T.P., Mizell, D.W.: Augmented reality: an application of heads-up display technology to manual manufacturing processes. In: Boeing Computer Services, Research and Technology, Seattle, WA 98124–0346 (1992)
31. Kato, H., Billinghurst, M., Asano, M., Tachibana, K.: An augmented reality system and its calibration based on marker tracking. Trans. Virtual Reality Soc. Jpn. **4**(4), 607–616 (1999)
32. Amin, D., Govilkar, S.: Comparative study of augmented reality SDKs. Int. J. Comput. Sci. Appl. (IJCSA), **5**(1) (2015)
33. Chris Bank, Gestures & Animations: The Pillars of Mobile Design. UX Magazine. Article No. 1351, 1 December 2014

Study and Comparison of Metadata Schemas
for the Description of Multimedia Resources

Angela M. Vargas-Arcila[1]([⊠]), Sandra Baldassarri[2],
and José L. Arciniegas-Herrera[1]

[1] Universidad Del Cauca, Popayán, Colombia
{amvargas, jlarci}@unicauca.edu.co
[2] Universidad de Zaragoza, Zaragoza, Spain
sandra@unizar.es

Abstract. In this paper, the description of the most relevant metadata schemas of multimedia content annotation for digital television are presented. The analysed schemas are: MPEG-7, TV-Anytime, P-META, EBUCore, PBCore, and SMPTE. For each of them, their most basic features are explained, and their extensions and application profiles for audio, video or audiovisual content are identified. Furthermore, the paper clarifies the characteristics and relationships between schemas, and checks their compliance with the multimedia content description requirements of television. Finally, there is a comparison between them, identifying advantages and disadvantages.

Keywords: Metadata schema · Multimedia content · Digital television

1   Introduction

The different services of digital interactive television (DiTV) are classified according to the service features, for the final user point of view, in: (1) distributed content services (broadcasting, on demand, publicity, time-shifting and place-shifting, and complementary content), (2) interactive services (of information, commerce, entertainment, learning, medical, monitoring, website and interactive publicity), (3) communication services and (4) other services (see Fig. 1).

In first place, the distributed content services are oriented to the broadcasting of content and are classified in: broadcast services, on-demand services, advertising services, time-shifting and place-shifting services, and supplementary content.

Broadcast services comprise a one-way transmission to two or more end users, where end users have no control over the content or timing of what they receive, apart from the ability to select a particular channel. Some services of this type are linear TV, pay per view, linear TV with multi-view, etc.

On-demand services allow to the end user select and retrieve content at any time, according to the constraints provided by the content protection metadata. Time-shifting and place-shifting services allow the access and control of the content without time or place limitations (pause, rewind, fast forward, etc.). And supplementary content refers to video, audio, text, graphics or other content that can be optionally accessed by users. Its features are: it only works in conjunction with the main content, and it is

© Springer International Publishing Switzerland 2016
M.J. Abásolo et al. (Eds.): jAUTI 2015/CTVDI 2015, CCIS 605, pp. 59–73, 2016.
DOI: 10.1007/978-3-319-38907-3_6

synchronous with the main content. For example, subtitles and captions, audio description, sign language interpretation, etc.

Secondly, interactive services allows end user to send different types of requests to service provider and receive feedback with interactivity. For example, information services that support multiple types of content, such as news, weather forecasts, etc., commercial services, entertainment service designed to provide content, such as games, karaoke, blogs, etc., learning services for delivering educational content, medical services, monitoring services and interactive advertising.

Thirdly, the communication services enable the end user to communicate with other end users via messaging, telephony, video calls or video conferencing.

And lastly, there are other services which cannot be classified in any of the above categories. These services are: public interest services (support for end users with disabilities, emergency communications, etc.), hosting services (for example: user created content hosting) and presence services (manage presence information between end-users: "watching television", "watching a football match", etc.) [12].

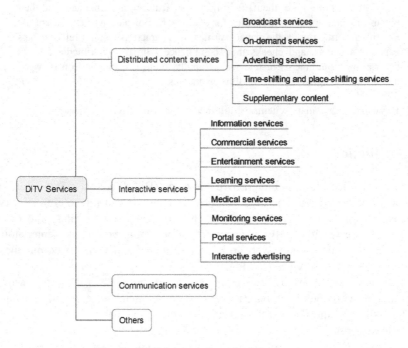

Fig. 1. Digital interactive television services

Although the TV viewer can use any of these services, the most often used services are: to select a program to be seen in broadcasting time or to record a program to be seen later. In order to make easier the selection of contents to the users, some information about them is needed: title, actors, genre and summary, among others. On their behalf, either the content or the TV service providers have to attract the user to their contents giving this information. As the data about the content the TV viewer wants to consume can be stored in metadata, these become very relevant [8]. In consequence, there are several sets of metadata specially aimed to the TV content annotation either as in a general or as a contextual way, that is, they describe any audiovisual content or particular contents as news, films, publicity, etc. These sets of metadata used to have a well-defined structure and a set of rules for it use called metadata schema. There are several metadata schemas for annotation of web and television multimedia contents; however, in the literature no reference to a review of schemas that allow to describe this kind of content in the television context independently of their creation scope has been found. For this reason, in this paper, the more relevant metadata schemas for the annotation of TV multimedia content have been classified, with the aim of explaining their connections and features and verifying if they fulfill the requirements of the description of television contents.

The remainder of this paper is organized as follows. Second section presents the theoretical framework of the metadata in the television context. Third section describes the most important metadata schemas in the annotation of television multimedia contents, which are deeply compared in the fourth section. Finally, the last section presents the conclusions carried out in this study.

2 Theoretical Framework of Metadata Schemas in DTV Industry

A metadata is known as a data about other data or information about information [15]. Metadata are defined as information that describes, identifies, explains or defines a resource for making easier its recovering, use or management. There are metadata sets that allow to describe a special kind of resource, since they are designed with a specific intention. These sets are called metadata schemas and they establish rules for its use. A metadata schema can be modified, firstly by adding new metadata (the result is known as "extension"), secondly by limiting and refining the use of available metadata, or mixing metadata from different schemas (the result is known as "application pro-file") [27]. In digital television industry, it is common the use of metadata schemas for describing the types of contents: films, news, publicity, etc., and for facilitating the management and interchange of these contents in different domains of the TV value chain. The general value chain of digital TV (DTV) in each of its types (terrestrial, over IP, wiring, satellite) is formed by four domains: content provider domain, TV service provider domain, net provider domain and consumer domain (see Fig. 2).

In the content provider domain the production, edition and elaboration of content metadata (films, events, documentary, etc.) is carried out. In this domain, the metadata include all the information related with the production phases: pre-production (e.g. scriptwriters, creative, etc.), production (e.g. costume, makeup, actors, cameras, etc.) and post-production (e.g. special effects, soundtrack, etc.) [2].

In the domain of the service provider the content aggregation is done, that is, the contents are prepared to be sent to the final user and the platform services (e.g. charges, user authentication, etc.) and the complements to enrich the TV service (e.g. com-munication services, interactive services, publicity, etc.) are provided. The content provider gives to this domain the contents with its metadata for making easier the

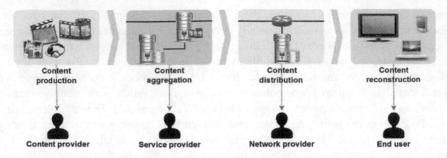

Fig. 2. DTV value chain

transmission and for avoiding a new description of the resource that can introduce mistakes in the information. However, the TV service provider can create metadata, especially administrative, or, if it is necessary, descriptive and structural metadata related with the content. Metadata allow this domain to create a TV programming guide properly and add services that take into account the semantic of the content, in order to improve the user experience.

In the value chain, the network provider receives the contents from the DTV service provider domain and gives them to the consumer domain, which is formed by the terminals and devices for the service consume (TV, computer, decoder, *Set-Top-Box,* mobile phone, etc.). These devices allow to receive and restore the contents in a suitable format for being displayed [17]. It is important to highlight that in the DTV value chain, not only the metadata to describe the contents are set, but also the behaviour of the user during its interaction with the television services, that are included in this last domain.

3 Description of Metadata Schemas for Multimedia Content Annotation

This work has considered different metadata schemas, extensions and application profiles that can be used in the digital television industry, such as, SMEF, MXF Metadata Schema, MPEG-7, egtaMeta, among others. However, it describes the most important and in force: MPEG-7, TV-Anytime, P-META, EBUCore, PBCore and SMPTE Metadata Element Dictionary Structure.

3.1   MPEG-7

MPEG-7 is a metadata schema for multimedia content description that allows to describe digital images, digital video or digital audio in a complete way [28, 20]. It was standardized in ISO/IEC 15938 (Multimedia Content Description Interface) by Moving Pictures Experts Group. MPEG-7 is focused on representing information about the content, and not on its codification [20] like other standards as MPEG-1, MPEG-2 and MPEG-4 [13].

Although it was not designed primarily for TV content as in the case of other standards, MPEG-7 provides a set of metadata related to conceptual information of reality captured by the content (actors, objects, events). It is capable of supporting a large group of applications because it has a generic approach; and different standards developed by other groups that are oriented towards specific applications were considered in its creation [3]. In addition to metadata generally used to describe multimedia content directly related to the production process (title, location, actors, etc.), the storage formats and copyright, MPEG-7 allows to add semantic information to the description of content (who, what, when, where, events, objects, etc.), low level structural information (forms, colors, textures, movements, sounds, etc.), and information related to spatial structure, temporal or spatial-temporal (scene cuts, segmentation into regions and motion tracking region) [13]. The information related to the temporal structure is an advantage of MPEG-7, it means that MPEG-7 has the ability to segment the content in the time and assign different metadata to each part [13], and allows to define different types of segments and to create hierarchies of segments [23].

Furthermore, its metadata are not presented as a list, but they are part of a hierarchical structure designed by metadata sets, as shown in Fig. 3. Metadata represented by "D" are named descriptors and represent a content feature [20]. Descriptors are grouped according to their function to be part of a description scheme (DS).

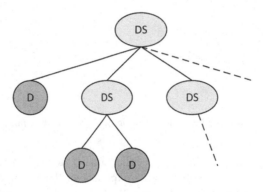

Fig. 3. Hierarchical structure of the MPEG-7 elements [20].

MPEG-7 uses the Description Definition Language (DDL), it is based on XML and allows the extension and modification of existing elements [20]. It also uses the concept of Classification Schemas (CS) to define a vocabulary for describing a domain as a set of terms. These terms may be used to assign a value to a specific metadata [10].

3.2   TV-Anytime

TV-Anytime (TVA) is a standard published through reports and technical specifications of ETSI (ETSI TS 102 323 and ETSI TS 102 822) that are referenced within the

ITU recommendations. Its creator is TV-Anytime Forum, a global consortium dedi-
cated to produce standards for television receivers and led by worldwide consumer
electronics manufacturers, broadcasters, telecommunications operators, etc. [3]. The set
of specifications that encompasses TVA aims to allow the search, selection, acquisition
and correct use of content in personal or local storage systems from online to broadcast
services, so TVA intended as a guide for manufacturers and television services providers [7].

The standard was developed in two phases and takes into account the use of
metadata to meet its objectives, therefore, TVA clearly defines a metadata schema for
audiovisual content, which takes its name. In the first phase, the metadata to describe
the audiovisual content, to set information about group and content segmentation or to
describe the user preferences, to add information about the supplier, and to set right or
privacy policies, are defined [8, 22]. The second phase extends the first one adding the
description data about the content and data about how the content must be consume [9]
(see Fig. 4).

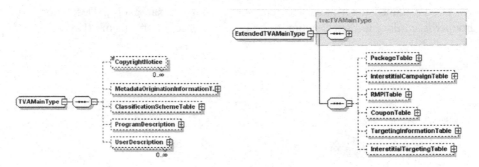

Fig. 4. TVA: Main elements included in phase 1 (left) and in phase 2 (right) [9]

In digital television, a package is a collection of items that are intended to be
consumed together to provide different user experiences. This is possible thanks to the
definition of packaging in the specification TS 102 822-3-3 of TVA that enables the
combination of different types of content items, such as games, applications, images
and text. Is important to highlight that the new introduced metadata in TVA Phase 2
allow describing the new content types in addition to the temporal and spatial synchronization information between elements of the package. Thanks to the synchronization information, TVA can provide multi-flow experiences with content packages
(for example: a game from different angles (multi-camera)) [8]. Another important in
the context of the television aspect is the Information Rights Management and Protection (RMPI), which includes elements TVA Phase 2 to allow the user to know the
rights associated with the content before purchase. The description of the content
through TVA is completely independent of the channel, schedule and broadcast protocol, to ensure this independence, the standard proposes to associate a unique identifier to each content called Content Regarding Identifier (CRID) [22].

TVA has chosen DDL as its metadata representation format, as MPEG-7 does [3], and uses the same philosophy of classification schemas to choose a value for a metadata within a set of possible values already defined.

This standard allows to describe audiovisual content, content packages, and content segments, allowing navigation within a piece of segmented content. Also, it has a set of metadata intended to describe user preferences and consumer habits that can be used by applications or software agents to search and select appropriate content for the user [3, 26].

3.3   P-META

Since 1999, the ECM MAG (Expert Community on Metadata - Multistakeholder Advisory Group) EBU (European Broadcasting Union) project group has been working on creating a standard vocabulary for information related to audiovisual products and audiovisual broadcasting industry, and has designed the semantic metadata schema EBU P-META known as P-META and defined in the specification EBU TECH 3295 (EBU Tech 3295 Technical specification). P-META was originally set up to support the exchange of content between organizations or production systems, but it has also been used as a set of descriptive semantic metadata [4].

P-META is a list of metadata focused on the exchange of commercial audiovisual products between broadcasters [14]. It also consists of a set of data types, syntax rules and a library of controlled terms [5] that should be taken into account when generating the metadata that will identify editorially or will describe technically a specific resource and rights associated [4, 14].

From technological perspective, P-META has been designed to be as flexible as possible in the implementation, because doesn't go beyond the definition of the terms and therefore can be materialized through different ways: as XML documents, Word templates and inserting metadata in file formats such as MXF (SMPTE 377-1-2009 Material Exchange Format) or BWF. In this way, P-META is independent of technology [4, 14]. It can be implemented just as defined in the specification or can be extended to meet specific needs. However, P-META is not intended to be used in database (although it could be used as a starting point) [4, 5].

3.4   EBUCore

The ECM MAG project group of EBU defined EBUCore in the technical specification EBU TECH 3293 as a metadata schema based on Dublin Core (DC) in order to maximize interoperability with the community of DC users and for this reason is known as the Dublin Core for multimedia. It is a set of descriptive, administrative, technical and structural metadata that allows to describe audiovisual content with the minimum necessary information and beyond enabling the description of the content in production environments. It can also be used to describe characteristics of distribution of that content [6].

EBUCore has been designed as a minimum and flexible list of metadata to describe audio and video resources for a wide range of broadcasting applications including archives, exchange and production. It is also a metadata schema with well-defined syntax and semantics for easier implementation [6]. It is currently in version 1.5 which takes into account the latest developments of the Semantic Web and Linked Open Data community, which is why EBUCore 1.5 is available in RDF. Some of the application profiles based on EBUCore are EBU ADM (EBU Audio Definition Model) and EgtaMETA. EBU ADM is described in the technical specification EBU TECH 3364 and provides a complete set of technical and information metadata to describe audio files. Today, it is already incorporated in the 3293 specification and therefore is part of EBUCore schema. EgtaMETA, meanwhile, is described in the EBU TECH 3340 specification and defines the syntax and semantics of structured descriptions for the annotation and exchange of advertising material.

Finally, is important to note that currently EBUCore has replaced the described above P-META specification.

3.5   PBCore

Public Broadcasting Metadata Dictionary (PBCore) is a free metadata schema, funded by the Corporation for Public Broadcasting of United States [18]. It is designed to be used by television, radio and web providers, and aims to be a standard way of describing and using the multimedia content in order to facilitate resource recovery and sharing between colleagues, software systems, institutions, production partners, etc. [13]. Since its launch in 2005, it has been adopted by many users that are part of the audiovisual industry and currently it is in version 2.0.

It is based on Dublin Core and adds a number of useful metadata for multimedia resulting in a lot of metadata organized in 15 containers which in turn are divided into 4 classes: instantiation, intellectual content, intellectual property, extensions [19]. It intends to be simple like Dublin Core and be a starting point for users to take it as a basis to create their own extensions [13].

3.6   SMPTE Metadata Element Dictionary Structure

Society of Motion Picture and Television Engineers (SMPTE) is an internationally recognized organization in the development of standards related to image, sound and metadata; its standard SMPTE ST 335 (Metadata Element Dictionary Structure) defines a large and complex metadata schema for audiovisual resources and is designed to cover the entire production chain [3, 25].

Metadata defined by SMPTE are classified in various hierarchically structured classes of metadata (see Fig. 5). The metadata classes are sets of metadata with common characteristics and attributes. This classification facilitates the management of metadata, provides flexibility in the capture and exchange of metadata between applications [25].

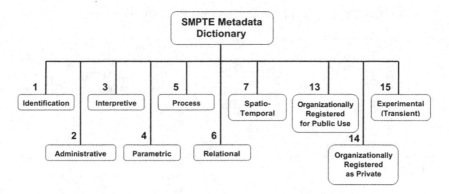

Fig. 5. SMPTE structure [25].

4   Relationship and Comparison Between the Metadata Schemas

Figure 6 graphically shows the relationship between the standards studied, highlighting those with the greatest impact in the context of television.

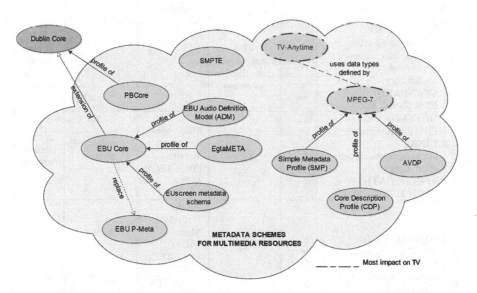

Fig. 6. Relationship between metadata schemas for multimedia content on DTV.

Table 1 shows a comparison between the previous metadata schemas through five elements. In the first column, the creator, the name of the standard or specification and the link is presented. The second column shows the metadata schema from which is an extension or profile. The third column shows if making metadata schema extensions is allowed or not. Columns four and five display the profiles and extensions of each

Table 1. Characteristics of metadata schemas for multimedia content on TV.

NAME	DEVELOP BY / LINK /STANDARD OR SPECIFICATION	BASIC METADATA SCHEMA	ALLOW EXTENSIONS	PROFILES/ EXTENSIONS RELATED WITH MULTIMEDIA		SEGMENTATION
				NAME	**APPLICATION**	
MPEG-7	**DEVELOP BY:** Moving Picture Coding Experts Group (MPEG) **LINK:** http://www.iso.org/ **STANDARD:** ISO/IEC 15938		YES (mainly through classification schemas)	Audio Visual Detailed Profile (AVDP)	audio, video audiovisual content	in time and space
				Simple Metadata Profile (SMP)	multimedia	
				Core Description Profile (CDP)	multimedia	
				PrestoSpace	news	
TVA	**DEVELOP BY:** TV-Anytime Forum **LINK:** http://www.tv-anytime.org/ **STANDARD:** ETSI TS 102 822		YES (mainly through classification schemas)			in time (limited description)
P-META	**DEVELOP BY:** EBU Project Group **LINK:** https://tech.ebu.ch/metad ata/p_meta **SPECIFICATION:** TECH 3295 (09/2011)		YES	EBU Music Reporting Metadata EBU TECH 3332	music	in time (limited description)
EBUCore	**DEVELOP BY:** EBU Project Group **LINK:** https://tech.ebu.ch/Metad ataEbuCore **SPECIFICATION:** TECH 3293 (04/2014)	**EXTENSION OF:** Dublin Core	YES	Audio Definition Model (ADM) EBU TECH 3364	audio	in time
				EgtaMETA EBU TECH 3340	publicity	
				EUscreen metadata schema	audiovisual content for tv web	

NAME	DEVELOP BY / LINK /STANDARD OR SPECIFICATION	BASIC METADATA SCHEMA	ALLOW EXTENSIONS	PROFILES/ EXTENSIONS RELATED WITH MULTIMEDIA		SEGMENTATION
				NAME	APPLI CATION	
PBCore	**DEVELOP BY:** Corporation for Public Broadcasting **LINK:** http://www.pbcore.org/ **STANDARD:** No standardized	PROFILE OF: Dublin Core	YES (by its metadata class PBCoreExtensions)			in time
SMPTE	**DEVELOP BY:** Society of Motion Pictures and Television Engineers **LINK:** https://www.smpte.org/ **STANDARD:** SMPTE ST 335		YES (only for experimental enviroments, by its metadata class Experimental)			NO
OTHERS	• SMEF (BBC) • MXF Metadata Schema					

metadata schema, of which have been considered only those that describe any audio, video or audiovisual content. The sixth column indicates which schemas can describe a segment of audiovisual content either in time or in space, those that allow segmentation in time use the same set of metadata for describing all the resource to mark a segment of it, for example, "gender" is a PBCore description metadata and thus also be possible to establish a genre for a segment.

Moreover, TVA and P-META don't allow segmentation in time as described above; on the contrary, they limit the metadata used for this purpose. For example, TVA allows the description of segments only with: title, synopsis, genre, keywords, links to related foreign material and list of credits, however, they have the ability to group segments with a particular purpose or similar feature and associate metadata to segment groups and thus they facilitate the restructuring of an audiovisual stream to provide to the user another way of interacting with the content [23].

On the other hand, a television content description model shall be able to represent the following concepts [9]:

(1) A simple programme.
(2) A programme with a number of different versions (e.g. edits for sex/violence/language, director's cut, etc.).

(3) A programme that has been divided into a number of parts for publication (e.g. a 3 h film shown in 2 parts on different days).
(4) A programme that is a concatenation of a sequence of other programmes identified as an aggregated programme.
(5) A series of programmes that can be ordered (e.g. episodes in a numerical order) or unordered and bounded or unbounded.
(6) A collection of series and individual programmes that have the same programme concept, i.e., a show (e.g. all series of "Only Fools and Horses" together with the Christmas specials).
(7) A publication of a programme that may have publication dependent attributes (e.g. a film showing as tribute to a recently deceased actor which would have a different description).

Taking into account that most of the specifications and standards studied are focused on the description of multimedia content for television, Table 2 shows which of the above requirements of content description satisfy the schemas, based on the documentation and XSD files definition (an XSD file (XML Schema Definition) describes the structure of an XML document. It is also known as XML Schema).

Table 2. Metadata schemas vs requirements of TV content description.

REQUIREMENTS SCHEMAS	1	2	3	4	5	6	7
MPEG-7	✓	-	-	-	-	-	-
TVA	✓	✓	✓	✓	✓	✓	✓
P-META	✓	✓*	-	-	✓	✓	-
EBUCore	✓	✓	✓*	-	✓	✓	-
PBCore	✓	-	-	-	✓*	✓*	-
SMPTE	✓	-	-	-	-	-	-

*Comply with the requirement but in a limited way.

Summarizing the above, the comparison presented in Table 2 evidence the metadata schemas that were designed for the television context and clearly shows which meet the requirements of description of TV content, hence, TVA and EBUCore standards are the most suitable for covering these requirements. Similarly, considering the literature review, we observed that within the set of metadata schemas whose primary focus is television content, TVA is the most widely used, especially in research works such as [1, 11, 21, 24, 29] among many others. Despite the above and that the essence of TVA is to describe the content that contributes in supporting customized experiences of the viewer, MPEG-7 is the standard most influential in the field of multimedia content annotation [22].

Consequently, the most suitable and used standards in multimedia content annotation for television are TVA and MPEG-7, however, the decision to choose a standard or another depends on the application context. For example, in some cases it is preferable the simplicity of TVA with respect to the complexity of the syntax of

MPEG-7, while in other cases it will be necessary to provide the television programs with substantial semantic information, and MPEG-7 will facilitate it [23]. On the other hand, in some cases it will be preferable to implement the simplicity of segmentation of TVA compared with MPEG-7 because of the physical and operational constraints of diffusion [16].

5   Conclusions

In this paper, a deep study of different standards and specifications that are used for the description of television multimedia resources is presented. After the analysis carried out, it can be said that the more suitable schemas are TVA and MPEG-7, since TVA satisfies the requirements of annotation of television contents while MPEG-7 is the standard with more influence in annotation of multimedia contents. However, it must be taken into account that TVA and MPEG-7 have opposed features that can represent pros or cons according to the situation in which they are used. Therefore, the selection of the suitable one depends on the application context: news, education, films, etc. The more clearly opposed features are: main objective, syntax and implementation, and segmentation. In first place, the aim of TVA is the definition of TV experiences while the aim of MPEG-7 is the description of multimedia resources regardless the resource environment. Secondly, the syntax and implementation of TVA is simple while MPEG-7 has a complex syntax and a tedious implementation. Last, TVA allows segmentation in time and with a limited number of basic metadata, while MPEG-7 allows segmentation in time, space and time-space through a large amount of metadata being able to provide more semantic information and to describe complex scenes.

Finally, the connection among the studied metadata schemas must be highlighted. PBCore and EBU Core are based in Dublin Core (DC). The first one is a profile and the second an extension of DC. Although P-META is recent (2011), EBU Core replaces it allowing the implementation of different profiles and extensions aimed to particular applications. On the other side, TVA has no specific basis metadata schema but it chooses DDL as its metadata representation format, uses the same philosophy of classification schemas and reuses basic types of data defined by MPEG-7 for it definition files. Finally, as MPEG-7 is the schema more used for annotation of multimedia contents, it is the basis for the development of different application profiles and extensions.

Acknowledgements. This work is supported by UsabiliTV project (Framework para la evaluación desde la perspectiva de usabilidad de los servicios para soportar procesos educativos en entornos de televisión digital interactiva. ID 1103 521 28462) financed by education ministry of Colombia through Colciencias, and executed by Universidad del Cauca. It is also partially financed by the RedAUTI project: Red temática en Aplicaciones y Usabilidad de la Televisión digital Interactiva, CYTED 512RT0461.

References

1. Blanco-Fernández, Y., López-Nores, M., Gil-Solla, A., Ramos-Cabrer, M., Pazos-Arias, J.J.: User-generated contents and reasoning-based personalization: ingredients for a novel model of mobile TV. Expert Syst. Appl. **38**(5), 5289–5298 (2011). ISSN 0957-4174
2. CINTEL, Documento final– dinámica sectorial, debilidades y retos de la generación de contenidos sobre diferentes plataformas v5.0.1, Bogotá D.C. (in Spanish) (2010)
3. Delgado, J., Llorente, S., Peig, E., Carreras, A.: Metadata and rights interoperability for content interchange between producers of TV programmes. In: Proceedings ELPUB2006 Conference on Electronic Publishing, Bansko, Bulgaria (2006)
4. European Broadcasting Union EBU, EBU– TECH 3295, P_META Metadata Library, Specification 2.2, Geneva (2011)
5. European Broadcasting Union EBU, "P_META", EBU Technology & Innovation– P-META, (s.f). https://tech.ebu.ch/metadata/p_meta. Recover 18 June 2014
6. European Broadcasting Union EBU, TECH 3293 EBU Core metadata set (EBUCore), Version 1.5, Geneva (2014)
7. European Telecommunications Standards Institute ETSI, ETSI TS 102 822-1 V1.3.1 - Broadcast and On-line Services: Search, select, and rightful use of content on personal storage systems ("TV-Anytime"); Part 1: Benchmark Features, Technical Specification (2006)
8. European Telecommunications Standards Institute ETSI, ETSI TS 102 822-2 V1.4.1 - Broadcast and On-line Services: Search, select, and rightful use of content on personal storage systems ("TV-Anytime"); Part 2: Phase 1 - System description, Technical Specification (2007)
9. European Telecommunications Standards Institute ETSI, ETSI TS 102 822-3-1 V1.8.1 - Broadcast and On-line Services: Search, select, and rightful use of content on personal storage systems ("TV-Anytime"); Part 3: Metadata; Sub-part 1: Phase 1 - Metadata Schemas, Technical Specification (2012)
10. Feng, D.D., Siu, W.C., Zhang, H.J., Zhang, H.J.: Technological Fundamentals and Applications. Signals and Communication Technology. Springer, Heidelberg (2003)
11. Hyun-Cheol, K., Seong, Y.L., Joo, M.S., Ji, H.J., Han-Kyu, L., Jin-Woo, H.: Development of advanced PVR based on TV-anytime. In: 2008 Digest of Technical Papers - International Conference on Consumer Electronics, ICCE 2008, 9–13 January 2008, pp. 1–2 (2008)
12. International Telecommunication Union ITU-T, Supplement on IPTV service use cases, ITU-T Y-series Recommendations – Supplement 5, Mayo de (2008)
13. Joint Information Systems Committee JISC, Metadata Standards and Interoperability, JISC Digital Media| Guides, (s.f). http://www.jiscdigitalmedia.ac.uk/guide/metadata-standards-and-interoperability. Recover 20 May 2014
14. Marcos, G.: A Semantic middleware to enhance current multimedia retrieval systems with content-based functionalities. Ph.D. Thesis, Universidad del País Vasco - Euskal Herriko Unibertsitatea, Spain (2011)
15. N.I.S.O. NISO. Understanding metadata, Technical report, National Information Standards Organization NISO (2004)
16. NoTube Project Networks and ontologies for the transformation and unification of broadcasting and the Internet, D2.1 Requirements analysis, Feb 2010
17. Open IPTV Forum, Specification Functional Architecture v2.2, Release 2 (2013)
18. Public Broadcasting Metadata Dictionary Project PBCore, "Abourt PBCore", About|PBCore (2011). http://www.pbcore.org/about/. Recover 19 May 2014

19. Public Broadcasting Metadata Dictionary Project PBCore, "PBCore Documentation", Documentation|PBCore (2011). http://www.pbcore.org/documentation/. Recover 19 May 2014
20. Peig, E.: Interoperabilidad de Metadatos en sistemas distribuidos, Ph.D. Thesis, Universitat Pompeu Fabra, Spain (2003). (in Spanish)
21. Qingjun, W., Zhihong, W.: Research into application of TV-anytime standard on digital televisions. In: 2nd International Conference on Artificial Intelligence, Management Science and Electronic Commerce (AIMSEC), pp. 6318–6321, 8–10 Aug 2011
22. Rey-López M.: Marco Conceptual y Arquitectura para el Aprendizaje Personalizado a través de Televisión Digital Interactiva, Ph.D. Thesis, Universidad de Vigo, Spain (2009). (in Spanish)
23. Rey-López, M., Fernández-Vilas, A., Díaz-Redondo, R.P., López-Nores, M., Pazos-Arias, J.J., Gil-Solla, A., Ramos-Cabrer, M., García-Duque, J.: Enhancing TV programmes with additional contents using MPEG-7 segmentation information. Expert Syst. Appl. Int. J. Arch. 37(2), 1124–1133 (2010)
24. Sotelo, R., Blanco-Fernandez, Y., Lopez-Nores, M., Gil-Solla, A., Pazos-Arias, J.J.: TV program recommendation for groups based on muldimensional TV-anytime classifications. IEEE Trans. Consum. Electron. 55(1), 248–256 (2009)
25. The Society of Motion Picture and Television Engineers SMPTE, Metadata Element Dictionary Structure SMPTE ST 335:2012 Revision of SMPTE 335 M-2001 (2012)
26. TV-Anytime Forum, "WG Metadata (MD)", TV-Anytime Website (2003). http://www.tv-anytime.org/workinggroups/wg-md.html. Recover 30 June 2014
27. Vargas-Arcila, A.M., Baldassarri, S., Arciniegas, J.L: Propuesta de marcación de contenidos multimedia educativos en entornos de IPTV. In: Proceedings of Interactive of Digital TV - Workshop of Webmedia (WTVDI - XX Simpósio Brasileiro de Sistemas Multimídia e Web) (2014)
28. Vivancos-Vicente P.J.: El estándar MPEG-7 InforMAS Revista de Ingeniería Informática del CIIRM Dep. Legal: MU-2419-2004, ISSN: 1698-884 (2005). (in Spanish)
29. Young-Guk, H., Beom-Seok, J., Bong-Jin, O., Yu-Seok, B., Eui-Hyun, P.: Effective encoding of TV-Anytime metadata using EXI. In: 2011 IEEE International Conference on Consumer Electronics (ICCE), pp. 455–456, 9–12 Jan 2011

Building a Basic Hardware and Software Infrastructure for Developing Ginga-NCL Interactive Applications

Iván Bernal$^{(\boxtimes)}$ and David Mejía

Escuela Politécnica Nacional, Quito, Ecuador
{ivan.bernal,david.mejia}@epn.edu.ec

Abstract. This work describes the software and hardware components that were integrated to structure a testbed for developing interactive applications for ISDB-Tb´s Ginga middleware. A basic structure of the testbed was outlined and later built incrementally. This paper focuses on the set of software tools that we developed which turned into the basis of systems and applications that were created. The testbed allows obtaining the code for the applications and their transmission for testing on actual hardware. The developed applications can be sorted out into four categories: natural hazards, environmental issues, higher education and the evaluation of telecommunications services. For sure the testbed has its limitations but it was setup under a limited budget.

Keywords: Interactive applications · Digital TV · Ginga NCL · Testbed · ISDB-T

1 Introduction

Most of the countries in South America adopted ISDB-Tb (International System for Digital Broadcast-Terrestrial, Brazilian version) as their digital TV standard. A relevant feature of ISDB-Tb is its middleware Ginga for creating interactive applications. One option is to use the declarative programming paradigm Ginga-NCL [1].

The development of interactive applications requires not only software tools that ease up the task of writing and debugging code, but also the infrastructure for the transmission of video and audio multiplexed along with the code and media resources needed for executing the interactive application in TV sets or STB (Set Top Boxes).

This paper describes the infrastructure that was envisioned as a didactic testbed for the whole process of developing interactive applications. A basic structure of the testbed was initially outlined and built incrementally by developing software tools and obtaining hardware components under a constrained budget. The organization of the of the paper is as follows: Sect. 2 presents the basic structure of the testbed; Sect. 3 describes both the tools for generating and analyzing streams holding multiple video signals and interactive applications and the transmission facilities to broadcast such streams; Sect. 4 mentions the available reception facilities; Sect. 5 describes the systems and tools that were developed to generate the NCL code; Sect. 6 revisits the

© Springer International Publishing Switzerland 2016
M.J. Abásolo et al. (Eds.): jAUTI 2015/CTVDI 2015, CCIS 605, pp. 74–89, 2016.
DOI: 10.1007/978-3-319-38907-3_7

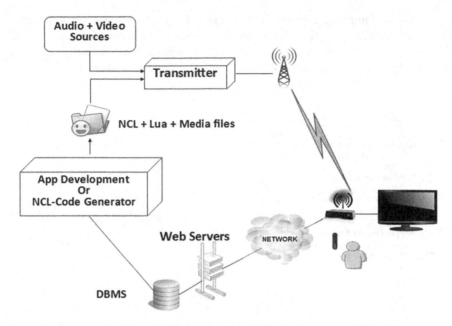

Fig. 1. Basic structure of the testbed

structure of the testbed and presents it in detail; Sect. 7 summarizes some results
obtained using the testbed facilities; finally, Sect. 8 outlines some conclusions.

2 The Basic Structure of the Testbed

The proposed basic structure for the testbed is presented in Fig. 1. The audio and video
source files corresponding to multiple programs must be multiplexed along with all the
required code and media files for the interactive applications; as explained in the
following section, the resulting stream is referred to as a BTS (Broadcast Transport
Stream) and this is what should be broadcasted. The NCL code must be written or
generated with the assistance of available development tools; some information stored
in a database can be included in the generated applications. In the receiving endpoint,
there must be TV sets and STB for executing the applications which may use the return
channel. The return channel can be used to send information provided by the user or
can be used to query data from a database and presented to the user. These operations
may require interactions with web servers.

3 Stream Generation and Transmission Facilities

3.1 Understanding the Meaning of a BTS

In ISDB-Tb, several programs can be combined and broadcasted in a 6 MHz channel
that was used by a single program in analog TV. Each program has video and audio

components are compressed by MPEG-4 and form Elementary Streams (ES) which are packetized and multiplexed to form what is called a Transport Stream (TS); this multiplexing process follows the MPEG-2 specification [2] and it can include other type of information such as tables that allow identifying each video or audio stream.

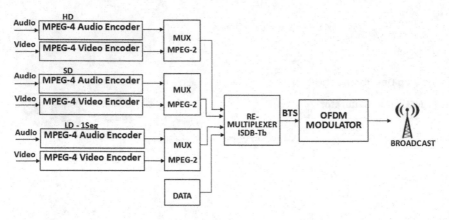

Fig. 2. BTS Generation

When combining several programs (re-multiplexing), each program may have different resolution; a particular configuration could be to multiplex a low resolution signal for mobiles (1seg), a standard definition (SD) signal and a high definition (HD) signal. All of these video and audio signals must be multiplexed not only with the information of interactive applications but also with information that allows the receptor to discriminate the information that belongs to each audio and video stream. A BTS is what eventually is transmitted. This is summarized in Fig. 2.

For obtaining a BTS, a Reed Solomon coding process is carried out in the transmitter by hardware, so what can be generated and analyzed at software level are streams previous to this coding, but we call them BTS in this paper anyway.

3.2   Generating a BTS by Software

For generating a BTS by software, the testbed integrates OpenCaster. LIFIA Labs from Argentina developed a patch for OpenCaster [3] in order to generate a BTS according to ISDB-Tb.

OpenCaster requires handling a set of programs that must be run in a specific sequence, each one with a bunch of commands and options that require the correct values. For easing up the task associated to the process of generating BTS, we developed a tool that employs a GUI (Graphical User Interface). In the background, the generator employs the user input and rewrites the scripts needed to generate the PSI/SI (Program Specific Information/Service Information) tables and the scripts that invoke all of the required programs. For this tool we employed two threads, one for handling the GUI and the other for handling all of the rewritten scripts. These two threads must be synchronized so that when the thread hosting the background processing finishes, it signals the main thread to notify the user about the end of the generation process. This tool was developed for Linux using Qt which is based on C ++.

The user has to decide the number and quality of each program and provide the associated video files along with the path to the directory hosting the application data (Fig. 3). The user can also customize several parameters for the BTS: name of the channel, area code, a name for the provider and service, PID for audio and video streams, etc.

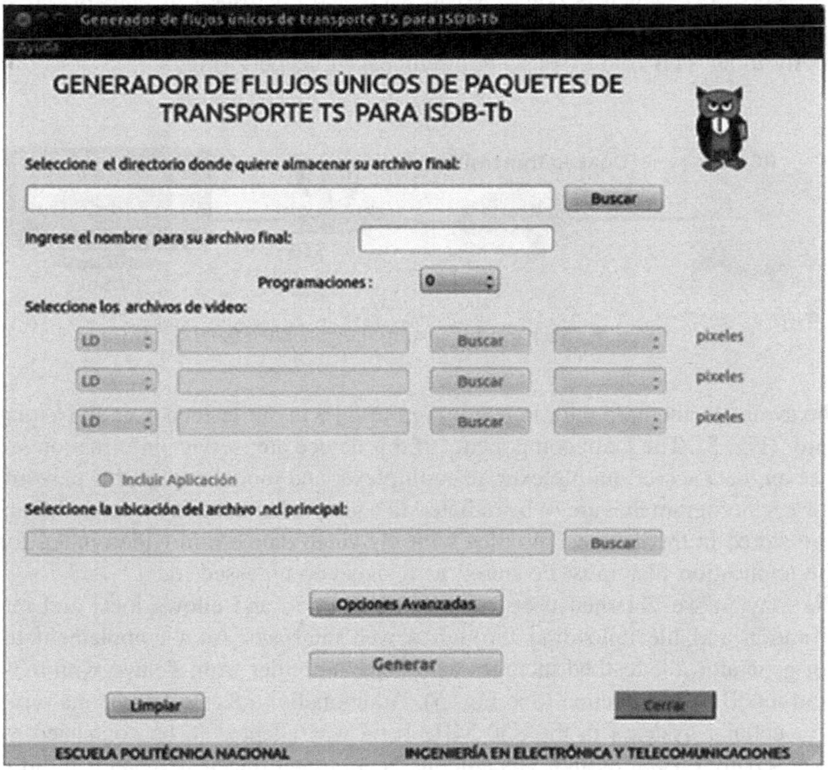

Fig. 3. Tool developed for generating a BTS by software.

3.3 BTS Analyzer

We also developed a BTS Analyzer [4] for complementing the graphical BTS generator. This new tool allows analyzing BTS containing streams corresponding to multiple programs and the code and media for interactive applications. The Analyzer was developed using Qt for a Linux environment. Once a BTS file is selected, the analyzer will process it and display information contained in each of several tables such as: PAT (Program Association Table), PMT (Program Map Table), SDT (Service Descriptor Table), NIT (Network Information Table) [4].

In order to develop such an application, it was mandatory for us to master the details of the aspects related to both MPEG-2 TS as well as BTS, focusing on the set of control fields, their functionality [5, 6] and the structure of PSI/SI tables.

3.4   Broadcasting the Generated BTS

BTS generated by our tool were tested by using a transmitter from DEKTEC, model DTU-215-I-SP [7], which is connected to a PC and controlled by StreamXpress for setting the transmitting parameters. The DTU-215-I-SP can be connected to an antenna or directly to an STB or TV set with an embedded decoder (Fig. 4).

Fig. 4. Scenario for testing the generated BTS.

The available alternative for transmitting our BTS in our testbed is an EiTV playout generator (Fig. 5). The main components of this device are: service information server, EPG server, data server, multiplexer, re-multiplexer and modulator. In this playout, the files for each program that are to be radiated in a given channel and the application files must be stored in the device. The files with the video data are provided in TS format and the application files must be stored as a single compressed file.

The playout we obtained uses a Linux distribution and allows local and remote configuration and file uploading through a web interface. As a complement to the playout generator, the testbed includes a 1 W RF amplifier from Telavo with a 30 dB gain and a 6dBi Yagi antenna (See Fig. 5). Additionally, a Kathrein antenna typically used for cellular systems in the 850 MHz band was adapted to be connected to the amplifier's output; even though this antenna is not tuned for the TV bands it did work and allowed us to increase the coverage range during our tests when using the highest TV frequency channels. Figure 5 presents a partial view of the final physical testbed. We obtained most of the hardware components of the testbed thanks to our participation in a national competition organized by the Ministry of Telecommunications (MINTEL). Our proposal was declared as the winner and received the playout generator, the amplifier, the Yagi Antenna, a TV set and several STB.

Fig. 5. EiTV playout generator, Telavo amplifier and Yagi antenna

4   Reception Facilities

Given the diverse features of STB and TV sets, it is convenient to have a set of different makes and models; for sure, it is not possible to include all of them. There is a wide range of possible combinations since there is the chance that the devices support or not: Ginga (Ginga-NCL or Ginga-J), Lua, the return channel (a LAN o WLAN port); they may have different amount of memory, USB port support, the way they manage memory may vary from device to device, etc.

Currently, we have TV sets (Sony and Samsung) with and without an embedded ISDB-Tb decoder and Ginga support and several STB. The make and models of our STB include EITV for development, VisionTec (VT7200), MundyHome (DEC-012B), CoraDIR, Pixela (PIX-BT108-LA1). We also use an old TV with just one coaxial input which requires a low cost analog modulator that takes as input the audio and composed video signals from an STB and delivers a modulated signal in channel 3 or 4; this is required since some families still use these old TV sets in Ecuador.

5   Application Development Facilities

5.1   Menu Creator: A Plugin for NCL Composer

NCL Composer, developed in Brazil, allows the creation of interactive applications based on Ginga-NCL and it is structured by a set of plugins that can extend its baseline functionality [8]. We have developed several plugins for NCL Composer that target easing up the development of interactive applications and are fundamental components of the testbed. One of the plugins favors the automatic generation of NCL code for menus and other for generating the NCL code for including an RSS feed in any application [9].

Composer is based on a hierarchical tree of NCL entities. This tree is structured according to the conceptual NCM (Nested Context Model) model and uses XML (eXtensible Markup Language), so that each entity is defined by a tag and may have child entities and may also become a child of another entity. Each plugin can manage the hierarchical tree of entities allowing the user to generate an NCL document without directly programming NCL code and providing a graphical interface (Fig. 6).

For managing the hierarchical tree of entities, a plugin must invoke the logic available in the composer-core (a basic component of the NCL Composer IDE) using the signal and slot mechanism which means that an object (an instance of the plugin) which wants to communicate with another must send a signal and the object which receives the signal (an instance of the composer-core) must connect the signal to a slot. A slot is simply a method that performs some functionality [10]. The plugins have been developed using Qt creator based on C ++.

We developed Menu Creator based on a hierarchical structure of classes (Fig. 6), some of them contain general properties of a menu such as the number of rows and columns, size and position of the menu on the screen, number of rows and columns that are shown in each view (a view is a fragment of a menu). Other classes represent: the text of the menu; two background images for when the menu item is selected or not; potential actions to be taken by the viewer through the remote control [11].

The hierarchical class structure adds NCL entities to the hierarchical entity tree so that the user can generate NCL code for each menu by using the plugin, as shown in Fig. 6. The plugin will generate an NCL context node for each of the designed menus. This context contains all of the details for the menu designed by the user [12].

Our plugin allows customizing several of the features of the menus and their functionality through a GUI such as the use of graphic styles, menus with different properties (number of rows and columns, size of the menu, etc.), splitting a menu in views, creating menus with rows and columns of different sizes, entering text, navigation between menu items and inserting NCL links [12]. When a menu is created, the name of a folder must be specified so the plugin stores the png images that it generates based on the entered text for each item.

Menu Creator: Navigating between Menu Items and NCL Links. When a menu is created, our plugin automatically generates the logic for the viewer to navigate between menu items and amongst different views, if the menu has been split. Besides, the plugin has a module for inserting NCL links. This allows the user of our plugin to associate menu items with each other or with other elements of the interactive application (e.g. media objects) through causal connectors [1], letting the plugin user to determine which element of the application to start, pause, stop or select in response to a specific action of the viewer through the remote control.

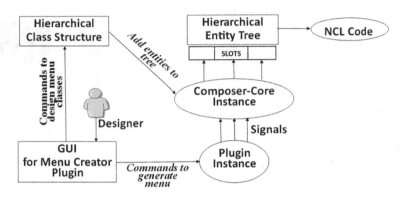

Fig. 6. Functional logic for the "Menu Creator" plugin

5.2 Menu Creator: Plugin Integration to the Testbed

The blocks in the lower left part of Fig. 7 shows a subsystem for searching, storing and processing information. The information provided by the web server infrastructure is included in the skeleton of automatically generated menus by means of our plugin "Menu Creator" and delivers interactive content.

For the subsystem we developed the following components:

- Two Windows Communication Foundation (WCF) web services; one that searches for information from websites, allows local interaction with the designer and interacts with the DBMS; a REST-based web service that is in charge of sending data from the DBMS to the viewer's STB or TV set using the return channel;
- A database for each interactive application that a user creates;
- An application to consume the web service allowing the user to perform actions related to searching, storing and processing of compiled information; and,
- An application, MIXER, that combines the information from the database and the menus created with the plugin to get the final interactive application in NCL.

By using the return channel, we decided that plain text is transmitted only to the user that requests it; in the STB, we format the information using Lua, an imperative scripting language that complements NCL. Our strategy reduces the size of the broadcasted application since images are no longer generated and transmitted for every piece of text.

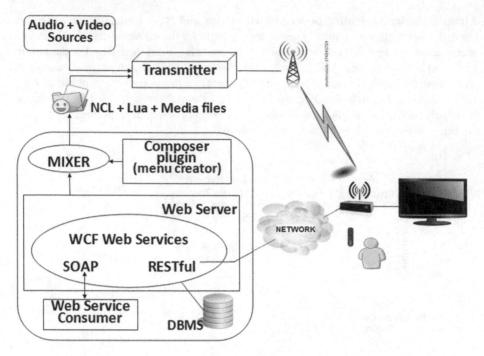

Fig. 7. Subsystem for generating interactive applications

5.3 A System for Generating Interactive Applications for Surveys

We developed a system for obtaining feedback from TV viewers regarding their opinions about mass services [13] as shown in Fig. 8; in particular, we applied it to evaluate the quality of telecommunications services. Our system consists of two main components:

- Survey Composer that lets users create and customize applications for surveys and automatically generate the NCL code that will run on the STB; and,
- A web application that manages the survey system in the server side, receives and storages opinions as well as displays the results.

Survey Composer was written in C# and the server side infrastructures was developed using PHP and MySQL. Survey Composer also generates the Lua code to handle the return channel for the interaction of the STB with the web server.

5.4 Additional Plugins for NCL Composer

We developed two additional plugins for NCL Composer, one for generating the NCL code for including an RSS feed in any application using the return channel to get the information from a remote server. The other plugin generates NCL code for applications following the paradigm of FAQ (Frequently Asked Questions), the return cannel

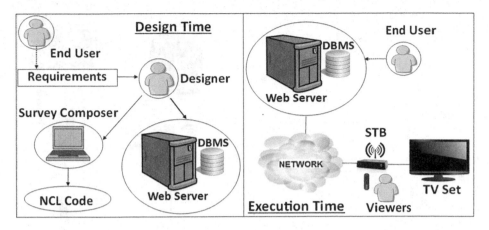

Fig. 8. Design and execution time of the survey generator system

is used to connect the STB to a web service which has stored a set of questions and answers. In both cases, besides the NCL code, Lua code is generated to handle the connection using the return channel.

6   A Complete View of the Structure of the Testbed

Figure 9 integrates the components that have been described through the previous sections and represents a detailed view of our testbed.

7   Applications Developed Using the Infrastructure Facilities

7.1   Information about Natural Hazards

We developed several interactive applications for informing local population regarding natural phenomena such as volcanic eruptions, earthquakes and tsunamis in Ecuador [14]. For determining the correct content of these applications, we looked for technical advice of the Geophysics Institute of the National Polytechnic School (IG-EPN) and the National Secretary for Hazard Management (SNGR). A main application was developed containing three secondary ones, the latter provide precise information about each of the natural phenomena mentioned above (Fig. 10). Additional applications for providing information about the IG-EPN itself were also developed.

7.2   Survey on Telecommunications Services

By employing the system for generating surveys [13] we developed a version for evaluating the opinion of users about the quality of service of their cellular provider. At design time, Survey Composer and the manageable web application were used to

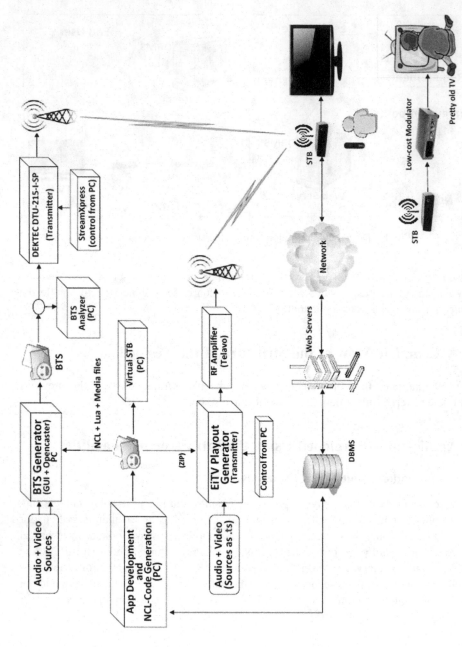

Fig. 9. Detailed structure of the testbed

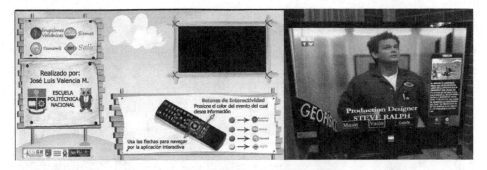

Fig. 10. Interactive applications about natural hazards and IG-EPN

Fig. 11. Interactive application for a survey about a telecom service

define the questions and the corresponding databases. At execution time, viewers interact with their STB or TV set and their opinion is sent to the server using the return channel to be stored in a database. The system presents the results of the stored information through a web interface and by generating a PDF report (Fig. 11).

7.3   Information about Higher Education

We developed several applications for informing TV viewers about diverse aspects related to Higher Education (Fig. 12) [9, 12]:

- The local ranking of Ecuadorian universities and general information about them.
- The program for competing for scholarships financed by the Ecuadorian government for attending international universities.
- For each university, the undergrad and graduate programs.
- The dates, requirements and other details about the general test that students must approve in order to get admitted into public universities.

Fig. 12. Interactive applications about higher education in Ecuador

7.4   Environmental Issues

We also developed several applications to inform and form viewers about recycling, environmental protection and ITT-conservation initiative using the elements of our testbed (Fig. 13).

Fig. 13. Interactive applications for recycling, environmental protection and ITT

7.5   Additional Applications

Based on demands of diverse sources, we developed several additional interactive applications such as one to inform viewers about the candidates for presidential elections and their proposals; information about MINTEL; an application for Yachay [9], a research city under development; an application about the Galapagos Islands and an application synchronized with the transmitted programming developed specifically for the IG-EPN (Fig. 14).

Fig. 14. Interactive applications for Yachay and the Galapagos Islands

7.6   MOS Scores

We used MOS (Mean Opinion Score) as a mean to evaluate the scores of several of the aforementioned applications from final user´s point of view. Consider as an example, the results of applying MOS to 50 subjects to evaluate the application regarding the scholarships to study in the best universities in the world financed by the Ecuadorian Government. Each item in the survey was assigned a range from 1 (bad) to 5 (excellent). Table 1 shows several of the questions and the mean value, median and standard deviation for the obtained scores. The values presented in Table 1 reveal that users have an overall favorable opinion about this particular application. Additional results of our application evaluations can be found in [9, 13, 14]:

Table 1. Mean standard deviation and median for MOS scores

Question	Mean	Standard deviation	Median
Does the interactive icon catch your attention?	4,08	±0,72	4
Do you consider adequate the size of the text used on the screen?	4,08	±0,78	4
Were you able to easily navigate in the application?	4,36	±0,66	4
Was the Help provided about how to use the remote control for navigating in the application really helpful?	4,16	±0,74	4
Do you consider that the application was easy to use?	4,14	±0,54	4

(*Continued*)

Table 1. (*Continued*)

Question	Mean	Standard deviation	Median
Do you consider clear enough the content of the application?	4,22	±0,68	4
¿Do you consider the elements that enable interactivity adequate?	4,4	±0,57	4
¿Do you consider that the interactive application added useful information to your knowledge on the main topic?	4,12	±0,75	4
Did you focus on the application rather than the normal broadcasted content?	4,28	±0,64	4
...	...	...	...
Total	**4,23**	**±0,68**	**4**

8 Conclusions

The testbed has become quite useful for the development of our interactive applications, specially the support offered by the plugins made the creation of interactive applications easier, at least for the ones that were developed. The development of the BTS generator and the analyzer demanded a deep understanding of some low level details of ISDB-Tb. Finally, it should be pointed out that the testbed was built incrementally and under budget restrictions.

The early broadcasting of digital TV signals in Ecuador started in 2014 and the development of interactive applications is in its early stages. We have focused on applications of public interest and meaningful for the Ecuadorian context.

Future work includes developing additional plugins for NCL Composer, systematic testing for the usefulness and impact of the tools we have developed, and additional testing for our interactive applications with end viewers in order to improve their usability.

Acknowledgments. The authors would like to thank to all the students that were part of our research group for their invaluable contribution to the execution of all the planned activities and that are partly describe in this article. The following students, now engineers, were part of our group, in chronological order: José Valencia, Gissela Cabezas, Fernanda Quezada, Fernando Becerra, David and Fernando Cevallos, Tatiana Moncayo, Mónica Pozo and Jaime Guzman. The authors also want to thank our university (Escuela Politécnica Nacional) and MINTEL for supporting our work. Special thanks to RedAUTI for enabling interactions amongst its participants which in turn have been an important support in our work.

References

1. Gomes-Soares, L., Junqueira-Barbosa, S.: Programando em NCL 3.0. Ed. Rio de Janeiro, Brazil (2012)
2. De Bruin, R., Smits, J.: Digital Video Broadcasting: Technology, Standards, and Regulations. Artech House, Norwood (1999)
3. LIFIA, OpenCaster 2.4. ftp://tvd.lifia.info.unlp.edu.ar/OpenCaster2.4
4. Pozo, M., Moncayo, T.: Generación del flujo único de paquetes de transporte TS de acuerdo a la norma ISDB-Tb y desarrollo de una aplicación para su análisis. Escuela Politécnica Nacional, Quito (2014)
5. VBrick Systems, Inc.: MPEG-2 Transport vs. Program stream White paper (2009). http://www.vbrick.com/docs/VB_WhitePaper_TransportStreamVSProgramStream_rd2.pdf
6. Asociación Brasilera de Normas Técnicas: Televisión Digital Terrestre - Codificación de video, audio y multiplexación, Parte 3: Sistemas de multiplexación de señales. ABNT NBR 15602-3 (2007)
7. DekTec - DTU-215. http://www.dektec.com/Products/USB/DTU-215
8. Azevedo, R., Araújo, E., Lima, B., Soares, L., Moreno, M.: Composer: meeting non-functional aspects of hypermedia authoring environment. Multimedia Tools Appl. **70**, 1199–1228 (2014). Springer
9. Becerra, F.: Diseño e implementación de aplicaciones interactivas basadas en Ginga-NCL para televisión digital en el área de educación superior. Escuela Politécnica Nacional. (2014)
10. Blanchette, J., Summerfield, M.: C ++ GUI Programming with Qt 4. Trolltech, Stoughton (2006)
11. Cevallos, D., Cevallos, F., Mejía, D., Bernal, I.: Sistema de Búsqueda, Almacenamiento y Procesamiento de Información para generar contenido interactivo de Televisión Digital. Revista Politécnica 33(3) (2014). Quito, Ecuador
12. Cevallos, D., Cevallos, F.: Diseño e implementación de un sistema de búsqueda, almacenamiento y procesamiento de información para generar contenido interactivo de televisión digital. Quito, Ecuador (2014)
13. Cabezas, G., Quezada, M.: Diseño e implementación de un prototipo para un sistema de generación de aplicaciones interactivas con Ginga-NCL para la evaluación de servicios masivos. Quito, Ecuador (2012)
14. Valencia, J.: Diseño y desarrollo de aplicaciones interactivas para el Middleware GINGA de televisión digital de la norma ISDB-TB para brindar información de los protocolos de prevención a la población en lugares de alto riesgo de erupciones volcánicas, sismos y tsunamis. Quito, Ecuador (2012)

IDTV Interoperability

IPTV Interoperability

Towards to a Usable and Accessible Mixed Global Standard DTT-IPTV

Carlos de Castro[1(✉)], Diego Villamarín[2], Gonzalo Olmedo[2], and Enrique García[3]

[1] Prometheus UTPL, Loja, Ecuador
carlos@cpmti.es
[2] Universidad de Las Fuerzas Armadas ESPE, Quito, Ecuador
{dfvillamarin,gfolmedo}@espe.edu.ec
[3] Universidad de Córdoba, Córdoba, Spain
egsalcines@uco.es

Abstract. This proposal includes the establishment of a joint standard for the integration of interactive open platforms: GINGA for interactive service on ISDB-T and Hybrid European standard HbbTV with SiestaCloud ecosystem for IPTV together. In addition, this standard will be interoperable with close or half open Smart-TV standards like, AndroidTV, AppleTV, AmazonTV, etc.; the incompatibility that actually exists between these platforms will be solved by this project. Our proposal also includes development of interactive applications on DTT and IPTV which assumes usability (SIMPLIT) and accessibility (W3C) rules. The authoring tool implementation is also contemplated for the development of interactive applications, under the concept of open existing access repositories templates and an extension of Unity framework for interactive 3D content development without having to program a single code line. Finally, a production methodology of audiovisual content (i-standardized, accessible and usable) in cultural, health, educational and commercial context will also be proposed.

Keywords: DTT · IPTV · iDTV · TDT · iTV · SistaCloud · GINGA · HbbTV · Interactivity television · SIMPLIT · W3C

1 Introduction

Nowadays the television has become one of the most important communication media and universities are called to propose alternatives to encourage TV good use, actually that means to take advantage of bidirectionality that offers the interactive digital television (iDTV) and to offer high quality audio, video and data, accessible, usable and intuitive, through educational, entertainment and social interactive applications. In contrast to analog TV, iDTV allows introducing data signal by which can travel applications (computer programs) to the receiver Set Top Box (STB) and the viewers are capable to interact with the issuer of the program (broadcaster).

For the Japanese - Brazilian standard ISDB-Tb, GINGA is the middleware for iDTV in Latin America countries [1, 2]. It is possible to show interactive content through IPTV broadcasting systems, and there are several platforms to get that, one of them is

© Springer International Publishing Switzerland 2016
M.J. Abásolo et al. (Eds.): jAUTI 2015/CTVDI 2015, CCIS 605, pp. 93–101, 2016.
DOI: 10.1007/978-3-319-38907-3_8

SiestaCloud ecosystem [7]. In other hand there is also a hybrid interactive standard HbbTV (Hybrid broadcast broadband Television) used in Europe [10–12].

International Standard for Interactive Digital Television, accessible and usable, SIESTA GINGA project is an initiative of the Universidad de las Fuerzas Armadas - ESPE, UTPL, the Center for Technological Innovation and Collaborative Entrepreneurship (CITEC) and CPMTI Company.

There is another initiative similar to our project, it is called GlobalITV, and this project Brazilian-European is focus on get the coexistence, interoperability and convergence between Ginga and HbbTV [10–12, 14]. They show some results of that, but they don't have a proposal to make an international standard, also we plant a platform more global and usable that also integrates IPTV and Smart-TV based on web interactive platforms, with an authoring tool for the easy development of interactive applications.

2   Technological Status

TV. Three generations of usability and convergence device on television can be defined now:

- The first generation is the conventional TV: it is unidirectional being watched from the time, it connects to the data stream.
- The second generation lets us control the time (synchronous and asynchronous). The user chooses (channel) in a similar way to conventional TV, but he can control the functions (Play/Pause/Stop/Rewind/Forward/Repeat) time execution of the content. It still remains unidirectional without interactive but may have multiple devices (PC/Mobile/Video).
- The third generation is coming now, multiple devices is maintained. It uses the Internet in the same way as the second generation, but it adds bidirectionality or interactivity. This means that both, the sender and the receiver take part of the program or data stream, as well, its conformation in space and time. People could interact through movements, gestures, voice, by touch, etc., from a remote control, PC, mobile, tablet or any other digital devices (microphone, camera, immersive system, virtual reality or augmented reality devices, etc.), with the content you are watching either video on demand pre-recorded and live television broadcast by the air or over the Internet.

IPTV. Internet Protocol Television has become the most common designation for television signals or video subscription distribution systems using broadband connections over the IP protocol. It is a complete system by which the television signal is delivered to users on the IP protocol (Internet Protocol). This system consists of content servers, managers to fragment encoding the signal and encapsulating the packets to be offered over the IP network using multicast or unicast transmission. The IPTV traffic can be protected from other traffic data to ensure an appropriate level of QoS (Quality of Services).

With continued improvements in the speed of broadband connection at home, the use of IPTV systems web-based TV, also known as Smart TV, are now increasing. These systems are based on a progressive download from a Web server, thus the user buffer is completed with the data until it reaches a sufficient limit, from which you can already play the video. These services live streaming, with a front-end playback on a web typically uses cloud computing technologies.

Ginga Platform. Middleware Ginga is located between the application code and execution infrastructure (hardware platform and operating system) that allows the development of interactive applications for DTT (Digital Terrestrial Television) regardless of the hardware platform and terminal access manufacturers.

Ginga-NCL provides a presentation infrastructure for interactive applications such declarative language written in NCL (Nested Context Language). NCL is an application of XML (eXtensible Markup Language) with facilities for interactivity aspects, spatial-temporal synchronization between media objects, adaptability, support for multiple devices and support the production of interactive programs nonlinear alive. NCL is a declarative language based on the structure defining a well demarcated separation between content and structure of an application, allowing structured define objects and related media in both time and space [3–6].

The interpretation of NCL code, rendering of content and control user interactivity are executed by the middleware Ginga. This was initially designed to run natively on Linux OS in production environments [9]. While there is a Windows emulation application, currently this is only provided for testing purposes within the scope of development and not as an application for end users.

HbbTV (Hybrid Broadcast Broadband TV). Is known like hybrid television (DTT + IPTV) because combine the terrestrial digital television advantages with the entire internet content, it can be video, photos, audios and interactive links. HbbTV is a global initiative aimed at harmonising the broadcast and broadband delivery of entertainment services to consumers through connected TVs, set-top boxes and multiscreen devices. The HbbTV specification is developed by industry leaders to improve the video user experience for consumers by enabling innovative, interactive services over broadcast and broadband networks. The specification uses elements of existing specifications from other standards including OIPF, CEA, DVB, MPEG-DASH and W3C.

The HbbTV specification was developed by European industry leaders to effectively manage the rapidly increasing amount of available content targeted at today's end consumer. It is based on elements of existing standards and web technologies including OIPF (Open IPTV Forum), CEA-2014 (CE-HTML), W3C (HTML etc.) and DVB Application Signalling Specification (ETSI TS 102 809) and DASH. The diagram shows the relationship between HbbTV and other existing standards. The HbbTV can work with either a broadcast or an IP link although it is most powerful when in a connected environment with a combination of broadcast and broadband networking [13].

Siesta Ecosystem. Siesta is an ecosystem of 3D 3I (Interactive, Intelligent, Inclusive) IPTV, result of a project funded with EUR 4.2 million by the CDTI (Spain) and the European Technology Funds, led by CPMTI, audited, evaluated and approved in Europe. It includes all kinds of local and cloud services within the same usable interface based on the use of six buttons or multimodal interactions (voice, gestures, touch, and movement) for interactive presentation of multimedia and IPTV content. Access to interactive digital content and services is performed through a light standard client (web browser), allowing independent use of hardware and operating system.

The Siesta digital ecosystem was developed on the premise that the software should offer the user a friendly and simple interaction. Siesta provides an interoperable, open and scalable environment that runs on PCs, tablets, smartphones and digital TV through an oriented interface for people with disabilities, elderly people, children, including technophobes [7].

Originally conceived in the context of the iDTV platform, Siesta [7] has evolved into a digital ecosystem formed by a set of applications, operating system and platform in the cloud that is the result of over 25 years of research and development led by EATCO group at University of Córdoba (UCO).

The original version of Siesta, designed to operate in iDTV is currently represented by the SiestaTV3D platform with support for Ambient Intelligence, bidirectionality and user interactivity with multiple services. This platform integrates the latest technological trends in human-machine interface systems and ubiquitous computing; cloud computing, interaction gestures, movement and speech, including the Internet of Things. The Siesta cloud version called SiestaCloud offers all Siesta capabilities through the cloud, including the characteristics of SiestaTV3D. SiestaCloud is a cloud platform services complemented by some Siesta operating system (SiestaOS) that can be installed on set-top-boxes (iDTV), SmartTV, desktops, laptops or tablets.

Interactive Digital TV Platforms Incompatibility. Actually each digital television standard has adopted your own interactive platforms, for example: DVB adopted HbbTV, ISDB-Tb adopted GINGA, Siesta and Smart TV for Web or IPTV services, most of this platforms are open source but also there are proprietor platforms and they aren't totally open because the manufacturers have their own developments and implementations.

Most projects on interactive digital TV platforms are oriented to the consumption of a particular type of content or services, whether for payment or sponsored being dependent on a specific device to access their interactive services, so this has produced a huge problem for the users and interactive applications developers, because this platforms are not compatibles between them.

3 Methodology (Siesta Ginga Project)

Faced with the initiatives showed in the technological status, in this work we present (Siesta Ginga Project) a response as a more globalized approach that seeks the full integration of the user with digital services and content of iDTV and with the services and Web 2.0/3.0 applications, as well as other advanced services in a mobility, multimodal, multilingual, and multi-channel context; in an accessible and usable way.

Figure 1, presents the general outline of Siesta Ginga project. Here we show an interoperable platform that will have common elements where the managements of interactive services with transparent interfaces will support any kind of content in different devices and the most important is that this platform will always have a usable guarantee.

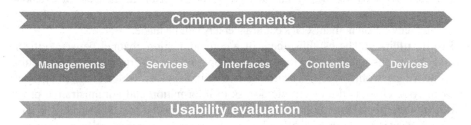

Fig. 1. General scheme of Siesta Ginga project

There are standards and rules of accessibility and usability as the W3C define by World Wide Web Consortium, the SIMPLIT certificate, Ginga and other ITU standards for interactive Digital TV, but none in general certifying that the systems developed satisfy the technical aspects of iDTV accessible and usable, with i-Standardized content (Communicability certification).

The objective of this project is the implementation of a new quality standard, certificated for the integration of digital interactive television platforms HbbTV, Ginga and Siesta considering SIMPLIT and W3C standards both for the applications development and services such as digital content production.

Also in the analysis of technical and commercial provisions it was evidenced shortcomings in existing products and services on the market claiming to be supplied with this project. There are isolated applications, and in other sectors applied, but not comprehensive and innovative solutions applied to the mixed iDTV (DTT-IPTV) as pursuing this project.

These shortcomings are understood as technological challenges to be solved during project development. Its current situation, our proposals for improvement, universities and industries who will lead such research, development and innovation and others challenges are as follows.

The differential value of this project is not only audiovisual applicability sector, because we can have applications and multidisciplinary services that can derive from developments in many economic areas like:

- **Health:** Primary care services will be provided where the physician will obtain data from patients, and these will find information. Non-invasive tests of simple demonstrations, such as ambulatory blood pressure, blood sugar, etc., will be made telematically. In addition, users will have access to diets, tips on food, prevention habits, etc.
- **Multimedia entertainment & TV:** A new distribution channel for many companies seeking new differentiating elements is created. In addition, having to comply with the accessibility and interactivity, it will be apt to reach all citizens without exception.

Demonstrators advertising (online ad buying clothes) and interactive games (board games and role-playing) will be made.

- **Culture:** The provision of cultural contents with high informative and educational value, coupled with the established status of accessibility and interactivity, offers a hitherto non-existent opportunity of bringing culture to all citizens with access to service television. All these services seamlessly link with regional and national mandate of extending broadband to all households. Demonstrations campaigns of cultural content and access to interactive content themselves cultural centers will be made.
- **Public utilities:** The establishment of a communication channel between citizens and the various public authorities will be supported to conform with the law requirements of electronic access for citizens to Public Services, which states the purpose of provide citizens the electronic access to information and administrative procedures, with special attention to the removal of barriers that limit such access. Demos carrying out procedures of public administrations and obtaining certificates, payment of fees, and several requests and inquiries will be made.
- **Training:** Allows the training and evaluation courses SCORM (Sharable Content Object Reference Mode) compatible and implements collaborative digital learning objects. Demos consistent in courses and training activities will be made in multiple formats (m-learning, e-learning, u-learning) and management training course itself [8].
- **Home automation:** Allows configuring the actuators installed in a house and they are compatible with the most economical and extended system possible. Demonstrator's management and home automation devices off, on or dim lights are made; opening and closing doors, up or down shutters, etc.
- **Smart-City & Internet of Things:** The Siesta ecosystem will be the core platform of ubiquitous city based on people and on increasing the quality of life of the same, allowing the interconnection of everyday objects with the Internet.

4   Functional System Features

The system will have the following characteristics:

- User dependence on fixed devices free, ensuring that user can consume under different standards services offered by the system, so multimodal and ubiquitous.
  - Multiuser, multi-standard and multiplatform system.
  - Multiplicity of profiles on data transmission, configurable on demand in real time.
- Proactive and adaptive capacity by combining several technologies.
  - Information retrieval systems and telemetry systems.
  - Artificial Intelligence, Ambient Intelligence and multi-agent systems.
  - Adaptive hypermedia systems.
  - New technologies of Web 3.0 and Semantic Web.
  - Recommendations based on data mining systems.
  - Customized systems.
- Management through Back-end tools integrated
  - Integrated production to different standards.
  - Provision of vertical services to different standards.

- Authoring Tool for easy interactive applications development.
  - Open access repositories with existing templates.
  - Unity extension Framework for interactive 3D development.
  - Make an interactive application using this authoring tool with no code line program.
- Cultural, health, educational and commercial audiovisual content has to be:
  - Standardized for television interactive applications.
  - Compliance with the more stringent requirements of usability and accessibility, primarily aimed at people with disabilities and elderly people.

5 Description of the Subsystems

The "**Advanced Siesta Ginga Platform**" is the central system to be developed, since it covers all aspects focusing on the contents related to the representation of scenarios, in everything related to the proper contents as all related information that must be transmitted between the different subsystems for get a correct viewing them. The system is

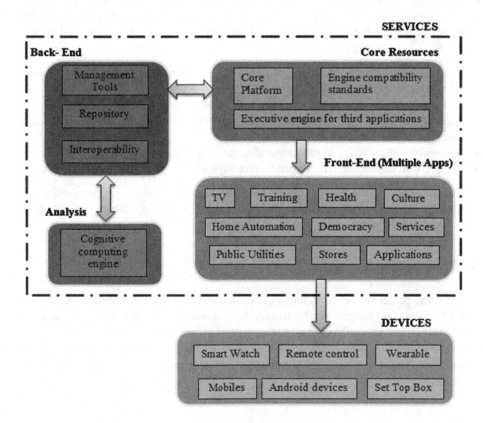

Fig. 2. Advanced Siesta Ginga Platform (Subsystems)

decomposed into basic subsystems that provide all the functionality to develop as detailed the Fig. 2.

Services: is the core of all services offered and contains all cross-platform services.

- **Core Resources:** has the ability to display 3D digital content streaming and on demand with integrated broadcast interactivity and social networks, ability to make recommendations to users, and ability to recognize and synthesize speech, ability to manage AAL (Active Assisted Living) interactive services, training or access to Public Administrations through a consistent and homogeneous interface like the presented in multimedia entertainment services.
- **The Back-End** of interactive services to manage platform aspects such as: scalability, load balancing, network settings, scenario settings, remote update system, service configuration system vs. display devices.
- **The Front-End** of interactive services allows vertical services consumption such as: TV and entertainment, education, health, democracy, automation, public utilities and access to the own applications store.
- **Analysis:** through cognitive computing engine allows deploy adaptive and personalized relevant content for each user.

Devices: the system includes various devices and peripherals that allow a final highly satisfying experience. To achieve this with the priority public platform to develop: children, elder, and dependent people, developed devices have to possess a high degree of usability and ergonomics.

- **Set-top-box:** Capable of playing fluently digital content on the platform as well as advanced services consume.
- **Remote control:** Endowed of six colored buttons, consistent with usable interface.
- **Mobile devices:** Capable of playing fluently digital content platform adapted to mobility and to consume advanced services.
- **Wearable:** allow users to monitor and access the content most suited.
- **Smart-watches:** allow a more productive access to the platform by advanced users.

In addition to these major subsystems, the need to develop synchronization and integration elements that enable smooth operation and collaboration between all subsystems must be included.

6   Discussion

In short, this project arises from the integration necessity of IPTV interactive platforms, HbbTV, Siesta and Ginga in order to establish an international standard for interactive digital television, accessible and usable in general with a series of vertical and horizontal service platforms, as well as the development of different types of author tools enabling automation of interactive multimedia programs production processes for DTT and IPTV.

Acknowledgements. This article was a result from the Prometheus stay in the UTPL in Ecuador of Carlos de Castro, with the collaboration of WICOM - ENERGY GROUP researchers of the Universidad de las Fuerzas Armadas - ESPE in Ecuador.

References

1. Ardissono, L., Kobsa, A., Maybury, M.T.: Personalized Digital Television: Targeting Programs to Individual Viewers. Springer Science & Business Media, The Netherlands (2004)
2. Baum, G., Soares, L.F.G.: Ginga middleware and digital TV in Latin America. IT Prof. **14**(4), 59–61 (2012)
3. Soares, L.F.G., et al.: Ginga-NCL: the declarative environment of the Brazilian digital TV system. J. Braz. Comput. Soc. **12**, 37–46 (2007)
4. de Souza Filho, G.L., Leite, L.E.C., Batista, C.E.C.F.: Ginga-J: the procedural middleware for the Brazilian digital TV system. J. Braz. Comput. Soc. **12**, 47–56 (2007)
5. Soares, L.F.G., Moreno, M.F., De Salles Soares Neto, C., Moreno, M.F.: Ginga-NCL: declarative middleware for multimedia IPTV services. IEEE Commun. Mag. **48**(6), 74–81 (2010)
6. ITU: ITU-T Recommendation H.761 > Nested Context Language (NCL) and Ginga-NCL for IPTV services (2009)
7. de Castro, C., et al., Anales de IIJAUTI 2013: Ecosistema digital Siesta y servicio de aprendizaje TV-Learning: Perspectiva para el escenario brasileño, p. 257 (2013)
8. Damásio, M., Quico, C.: T-learning and interactive television edutainment: the Portuguese case study. In World Conference on Educational Multimedia, Hypermedia and Telecommunications, EDMEDIA 2004, vol. 1, pp. 4511–4518 (2004)
9. Sotelo, R., Blanco-Fernández, Y., López-Nores, M., Gil-Solla, A., Pazos-Arias, J.J.: TV program recommendation for groups based on multidimensional TV-anytime classifications. IEEE Trans. Consum. Electron. **55**(1), 248–256 (2009)
10. Chicaiza, A., Meloni, L.P.: Implementation analysis of hybrid functions adapted to SBTVD and HbbTV. In: IEEE COLCOM (2015)
11. Dos Santos, M.R.; Calixto, G.M., de Paula Costa, L.C., Zuffo, M.K.: Interoperability analysis for Ginga-NCL and HbbTV application players. In: 2015 IEEE International Conference on Consumer Electronics (ICCE) (2015)
12. Moreira Calixto, G.; Keimel, C., de Paula Costa, L.C., Merkel, K., Zuffo, M.K.: Analysis of coexistence of Ginga and HbbTV in DVB and ISDB-Tb. In: 2014 IEEE Fourth International Conference on Consumer Electronics. Berlin (ICCE-Berlin), 7–10 September 2014, pp. 83–87 (2014)
13. HbbTV Overview (2015). http://www.hbbtv.org/. Accessed Feb 2016
14. GLOBAL ITV Project (2015). http://www.globalitv.org. Accessed Feb 2016

IDTV User Experience

A UX Evaluation Approach for Second-Screen Applications

Jorge Abreu, Pedro Almeida[(⊠)], and Telmo Silva

University of Aveiro - Digimedia, Aveiro, Portugal
{jfa, almeida, tsilva}@ua.pt

Abstract. Technological devices surrounding the television are changing, leading to changes in viewers' habits and to the development of second-screen applications created to provide better TV viewing experiences. Used while watching television, the 2ND VISION application presented in this paper is able to identify – through audio-fingerprint – content being displayed on the TV screen and present enhanced information on the second-screen. Under a participatory design approach, the development of the application took in consideration the users' opinion regarding its main functionalities and interface solutions and included evaluation test sessions conducted in laboratory settings. This paper reports on the adopted UX evaluation approach where opinions regarding instrumental, non-instrumental and emotional impact of the application were collected with a combination of SUS, AttrakDiff and SAM scales.

The results show that users experienced no major navigation problems and part of the iconography was validated. Considering the main goals of the application users were satisfied and interested in having such an application for providing additional information about the TV shows they watch. In addition the consistent variation of results between two sets of evaluation sessions, shows that the adopted UX evaluation approach is suitable to be used in a participatory design development of second-screen applications.

Keywords: Second-screen · Interactive television · User experience · Usability · Evaluation methodologies

1 Introduction

As technological devices surrounding the television changed, so have viewers' habits with the general TV experience no longer narrowed to a single and fixed location (typically a shared space at home) but extending to new locations and integrating different platforms. Mobile devices (smartphones and tablets) are being used not only as additional platforms for watching video contributing for the "space shifting" phenomenon [1] but also as companion devices, allowing for a greater involvement with what is being watched on (a regular) TV – e.g. by performing general web searches or to search for additional information related with the program being watched [2].

This is a consequence and simultaneously a stimulus for the focus of the Interactive Television (iTV) industry on the development of second-screen applications, designed to deliver supplementary information related with the TV content [3]. In fact, and

© Springer International Publishing Switzerland 2016
M.J. Abásolo et al. (Eds.): jAUTI 2015/CTVDI 2015, CCIS 605, pp. 105–120, 2016.
DOI: 10.1007/978-3-319-38907-3_9

mainly due to the ubiquitous character of mobile technologies, the opportunity for well-designed mobile applications and services to influence positively on individuals' day lives increases [4]. Nevertheless, and for this to happen, it is necessary to look beyond the product's usability [5] and start to consider the impact of emotions and aesthetics in the overall user experience of the system.

In this paper, the authors report on the 2NDVISION companion App to be used while watching TV, being able to automatically identify content displayed on the television screen and presenting related synchronized (using audio fingerprint) information. Conducted under a participatory design approach, the development of the application took into consideration the users' opinion towards functionalities, aesthetic and appraisal of the system.

After establishing the theoretical background (in Sect. 2 of the paper), Sect. 3 introduces the application main features and system architecture and addresses the methodological approaches that were taken during the iterative, and participatory development process, namely the first set of tests carried to validate a preliminary prototype in three dimensions and the evaluation of the final prototype, considering: instrumental qualities, non-instrumental qualities and emotional reactions. Finally, Sect. 4 presents the research results; and Sect. 6 discusses a set of conclusions related to the User Experience (UX) evaluation process that can be useful to other researchers, designers and developers of such kind of second-screen apps.

2   State of the Art

2.1   Second-Screen Applications

The growing success of second-screen devices is changing the way users relate and interact with the television. Using second-screen devices while watching TV is an increasingly common activity: according to recent numbers of Nielsen Company [6], 62 % of North Americans and 44 % of European consumers used second-screen devices while watching TV. Consumers are increasingly adopting a lean forward approach to the television experience, using connected devices as extensions of the program they are watching [6].

Secondary Screen applications are, in the context of 2NDVISION project and according to the description of Red Bee Media [7], those that provide a companion experience, aiming to increase and synchronously improve the viewer experience with content related to what is being displayed in the TV. By synchronizing the App with the television content, it is possible to provide enhanced-information (e.g. biographical data on a given actor, the name of the song that is playing, more details on the narrative of a series or film) or trigger events correlated with what is happening on TV, particularly in the context of interactive advertising.

Existing mobile apps perform synchronization with the TV content essentially based on audio fingerprint systems. This technology, which has collected the public recognition through applications such as Shazam (http://www.shazam.com), allows audio monitoring regardless of its format and without the need for meta-data or watermarks [8]. It is therefore possible to associate certain "signatures" or patterns to the audio providing or triggering events correlated with what the user is watching on TV. Given the increasing processing power of mobile devices, the evolution of algorithms and cloud-computing techniques, it is possible to use methods of image content recognition that, in essence, allow, on the one hand, to compensate the inherent limitations in the audio fingerprint and on the other, to open up new possibilities and use cases in the field of the secondary screen apps.

In this context, several applications have been developed, in particular for the US market, exploiting the synchronization capabilities with the content being displayed on TV. Again Shazam is an example, but also applications such as Viggle or Beamly. However, despite the above context, the specific offer for the European market (namely Portugal) is limited and 2NDVISION may contribute to enrich the Portuguese TV ecosystem with an end-to-end system allowing the app to synchronize (using audio fingerprint) and enrich both linear and non-linear (e.g. Catch-up TV or VoD) TV content.

2.2 UX in Second-Screen Scenarios

The specificities of mobile devices created numerous and significant challenges in the field of user experience – globally defined according to ISO 9241-110:2010 (clause 2.15) as: "a person's perceptions and responses that result from the use and/or anticipated use of a product, system or service" [9]. Mobile context, multimodality, connectivity, small screen size, different display resolutions and power emerged as factors to be taken into consideration when designing interfaces for mobile devices [4, 10]. Interacting with these devices implies a different look at user experience. User's hands are no longer over the mouse but directly interacting with the interface through multi-touch gestures such as swipe, pinch, press and hold [11, 12], creating the need for bigger buttons (to solve the "fat-finger" problem), wider distance between icons and new navigation paradigms.

Mobile usability models often focus on the effectiveness, efficiency and satisfaction, disregarding the cognitive load and the emotional impact of interacting with applications in no-longer defined time and place. When developing second-screen applications designed to enhance the TV viewing experience, these and other factors influencing the UX deserve a special attention.

3 The 2NDVISION App

The growing adoption of second-screen devices while watching TV emphasized the importance of developing solutions able to balance the user's attention between two or more sources of information (e.g. the TV screen and the mobile phone or tablet screen), namely by creating applications able to deliver additional content in a ease and user-friendly way. When developing solutions towards the user's engagement in the TV viewing experience, designers must take into consideration the pragmatic and non-pragmatic dimensions of the system. Usability is then a key issue as it is imperative to achieve a balance between the information in the first and in the second-screen minimizing the dispersion of attention [13]. Nevertheless, it is also important to consider the overall appraisal of the application [14] and its user experience, making it imperative to consider users' opinion during the design and development of the product.

These considerations were taken into account when developing the second-screen application reported on this paper.

Based in audio fingerprint, the developed app (2NDVISION) is able: to automatically identify content displayed on the TV and present related synchronized information (hereafter defined as markers, i.e. pieces of information composed by images, text and links for related sources of information); to automatically aggregate all markers in a sequential index; and to trigger notifications whenever new markers are displayed. Users could also save (bookmark), rate, filter and share markers; configure notifications to be triggered when new content is detected; and select programs to follow.

3.1   System Architecture

The 2NDVISION is based on an Event-Driven Architecture (EDA), which meets high performance in real-time events, immediate action to the consumers, "fire & forget" integration and a quality of service with the shortest waiting time possible (Fig. 1).

This architecture is composed by several modules namely the Automatic Content Recognition (ACR) which gears the second-screen device with the ability to perceive the content which is being visualized; and via the indexed markers by the ACR module, the solution has a Recommendation Engine that is responsible for the creation of additional contents.

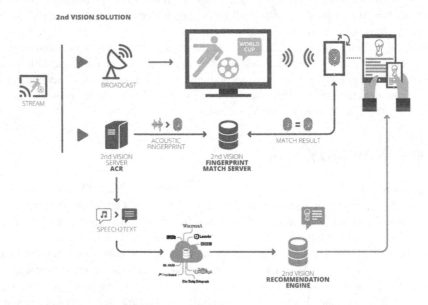

Fig. 1. 2NDVISION recognition and recommendation architecture

An Audience Engager module is responsible for obtaining user profiles through their interaction with the solution; and through the Advertising and Campaign Planning Engine it becomes possible to manage campaigns and advertisements related to the indexed content. In order to guarantee the persistent and in cache content management, the Content Repository module uses relational and non-relational systems for data management. The Back Office is the module responsible for the configuration of the solution, for matching the requests between the app and the content, markers configuration, image processing, users profile configuration and statistical reports generation. It is also possible, via the Gamification Engine to attribute a gamming environment to the 2NDVISION app and generate quizzes, polls and leaderboards, among other forms of user engagement. Finally, the Client Gateway is the communication channel between the APIs and allows the interaction between the mobile app and the backend of the solution.

3.2 Features

The 2NDVISION system architecture enables offering its users a wide range of features. This allows the structuring of the application in several areas. The following figure (Fig. 2) identifies 6 of the 8 areas/features available in the 2NDVISION App.

1. **Synchronize**: Triggering the automatic identification of the TV show being aired provides related and synchronized markers;
2. **Filter**: Content filtering categories. Example: Places (location, architecture, scenic spots, weather);

Fig. 2. The 2NDVISION interface - main screen

3. **Rate**: User's classification of the additional information displayed;
4. **Share**: Sharing any marker via social networks and e-mail;
5. **Bookmark**: Archiving of detected content for later viewing;
6. **Feed**: Area that displays the additional information related with the TV program (markers).

4   UX Evaluation Approach

4.1   Test Settings

As it was established that all the application design and development would be conducted under a participatory design approach, the research team carried test-sessions aiming to evaluate users' perception about the application instrumental and non-instrumental qualities, as well as their emotional reactions to the system. The first evaluation session, was carried in March 2015 by introducing evaluators with a first prototype of the 2NDVISION application (Fig. 3). The prototype allowed users to explore the most relevant features that were designed for the application.

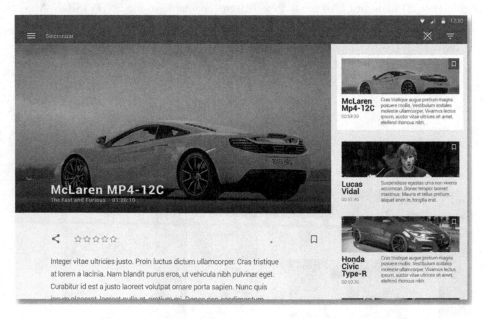

Fig. 3. The prototype used in the first evaluation session

The second and final evaluation of the prototype occurred in June 2015. Between the first and the second test session, some of the prototype's main areas were redesigned in order to reflect the opinions and inputs provided by the first group of evaluators (see Fig. 4). The functionalities of the prototype were extended with a context-advertising feature.

Fig. 4. Adaptations made to the application feed screen between March 2015 (image on the left) and June 2015 (image on the right)

Tests sessions were conducted individually in laboratory settings replicating a regular living room. Aiming to analyze the usability of the application the main goals of the tests were: (i) to evaluate the graphical interface; (ii) to validate the consistency of the adopted solutions (icons, layout and content organization); (iii) to identify critical interface issues. As far the user experience, tests were designed in order to evaluate the instrumental qualities (e.g. controllability, effectiveness, learnability) of the application; the non-instrumental qualities (e.g. aesthetics, identification); and the emotional impact on potential users.

4.2   Evaluation Procedure

Both test sessions (of the first and second releases of the prototype) followed similar evaluation procedures structured in three main stages. In the first stage, after a brief introduction to the application goals, each participant was left alone to freely explore the application for a few minutes. In the second stage, participants were informed about the structure of the test session and with the support of a pre-prepared video feed and related markers (triggered with an interval of 30 s) they were then invited to perform a set of tasks mainly focused on navigation (e.g. navigating between markers, exploring the index); iconography (e.g. correspondence between the icon and the related action); and in the use of specific features (e.g. saving, rating and sharing markers, scheduling programs in order to receive notifications). The third stage was the most relevant for the evaluation of the user experience. This consisted of a new free exploration phase supported by a dynamic video feed of three looped segments: TV news program (with a duration of 3'21"); iPhone add (30"); and IMDB Top Ten show (7'). At the end, a short interview was conducted and each participant was asked to answer three questionnaires.

It is worth to refer that being the second release of the prototype closer to the final version of the application the participants (Group #2) were allowed to freely explore the app and interact with its features after the completion of the referred tasks.

All tasks were performed under a cognitive walkthrough approach, and all data was recorder. After performing the tasks, and taking the CUE-model [14] as a framework and following adaptations mentioned in the UX considered literature (cf. ([15–18]), three instruments were used in order to assess the users' perspectives about the application instrumental and non-instrumental qualities, and the users' emotional reactions to the whole experience.

For assessing the application instrumental qualities (e.g. controllability, effectiveness, learnability), the research team used the SUS - System Usability Scale [19] and the Pragmatic dimension of AttrakDiff [20] (see Fig. 5). The SUS-scale [19] is a 10-item questionnaire with a 5-point Likert scale developed to assess several usability aspects such as ease of use and usefulness. As for AttrakDiff [21], it is an instrument created to measure the user experience beyond the instrumental task-based approach, by presenting the user/evaluator with three groups of semantic differentials. It also records the perceived pragmatic quality, hedonic quality and the attractiveness of an interactive product or application.

For accessing non-instrumental qualities (e.g. aesthetics, identification) the research team used the AttrakDiff Hedonic dimension.

Finally, for the evaluation of emotional reactions (valence, arousal, and control of the application), the research team used the SAM - Self-assessment Manikin [22]. The SAM-Manikin is a non-verbal pictorial assessment method that directly assesses the pleasure, arousal, and dominance associated with the user's affective reactions to a certain stimuli. The attractiveness value obtained from the Attrakdiff was also considered under this emotional dimension.

Qualitative data was also collected through the referred semi-structured interview conducted at the end of the test sessions, aiming to get the participant's opinion regarding the application (its main features), the interface and the adopted solutions.

4.3 Participants

Thirty-eight individuals (23 male, 15 female) participated in the tests sessions, 18 in the first session (March 2015) and 20 in the second session (June 2015).

Participants of the first session (hereafter referred to as "Group #1") were aged between 19 and 39 years old (age average = 28,1); 10 male, 8 female; 12 were attending or had already finished graduation courses, 4 had a Master Degree and 2 a PhD; 5 were full-time students, 4 were programmers, 2 were researchers and 2 were lecturers, 1 was a designer and 4 had other jobs or occupations. Regarding Television viewing and second-screen usage habits, 16 (89 %) mentioned to regularly watch programs on the TV, 13 (72 %) mentioned to use second-screen apps to search for information related with TV programs and 17 (94 %) mentioned to share content related with TV shows on social networking sites.

As for participants of the second test session (hereafter referred to as "Group #2"), they were aged between 21 and 39 years old (age average = 30,3); 13 male, 7 female; 16 were attending or had already finished graduation courses, 1 had a master degree and 3 had a PhD; only 4 were full-time students, 2 were programmers, 2 were researchers and 2 were designers, 2 were lecturers and 7 had other jobs or occupations. Regarding Television viewing and second-screen usage habits, 16 (80 %) mentioned to regularly watch programs on the TV, 9 (45 %) mentioned to use second-screen apps to

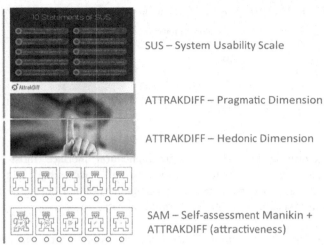

application instrumental qualities (e.g. controllability, effectiveness, learnability)

SUS – System Usability Scale

ATTRAKDIFF – Pragmatic Dimension

non-instrumental qualities (e.g. aesthetics, identification)

ATTRAKDIFF – Hedonic Dimension

emotional reactions (valence, arousal, control of the application + ATT)

SAM – Self-assessment Manikin + ATTRAKDIFF (attractiveness)

Fig. 5. Data collection: UX goals versus instruments

search for information related with TV programs and 5 (25 %) mentioned to share content related with TV shows on social networking sites. Nine of the 20 participants in the second test session had already tested the application in the first test session, that is, they were evaluating the application for the second time and for sake of a detailed comparison between the results of both sessions were considered as a control group (see section Discussion and Conclusions).

4.4   Results

As mentioned above, the prototype was developed under a UX approach and took into consideration the CUE-Model proposed by Mahlke and Thuring [14] to collect the participants' opinions about the application. Instrumental and non-instrumental qualities and the participants' own emotional reactions towards the prototype were evaluated by three different instruments: the SUS-Scale, the AttrakDiff scale and the SAM-Manikin scale (cf. Fig. 5).

Group #1. In terms of instrumental qualities (assessed through the SUS scale and the Pragmatic dimension – PQ - of AttrakDiff), data analysis (see Table 1) shows that when evaluated by the 18 participants of Group #1, the prototype scored 77,1 (in a maximum of 100) in the SUS scale, and 1,1 (in a maximum of 3) in the Pragmatic dimension of AttrakDiff. This means that, at that development stage, the application already had a good level of usability [23] but there was room for improvement in what concerns its pragmatic qualities. This conclusion was consistent with the data collected through interviews: when asked to share their opinion regarding the application and its main functionalities, participants pointed that it was an "interesting" application, namely by its ability to automatically present content related with TV programs.

Table 1. Application score according to the SUS, SAM and AttrakDiff instruments (Group #1)

Instrumental qualities	Non-instrumental qualities			Emotional Reactions			
SUS (0 to 100)	AttrakDiff (-3 to 3)			SAM (1 to 9)			AttrakDiff (-3 to 3)
	PQ	HQ-S	HQ-I	Sat.	Mot.	S. of C.	ATT
77,1	1,1	0,8	0,9	7,3	6,1	7,1	1,3

Regarding the usability of the application interface, most participants described it as "easy to use", "intuitive", "interesting", "accessible" and "well organized". Nevertheless this global opinion, participants pointed out some aspects that needed to be improved, namely the size (dimension) of some icons.

Non-instrumental qualities (closely related with visual aesthetics and identification) were evaluated through the Hedonic Quality – Identity (HQ-I) and Hedonic Quality – Stimulation (HQ-S) dimensions of the AttrakDiff instrument. On AttrakDiff, HQ-S indicates to what extent the product can satisfy user's need for novelty, interest and stimulation, while HQ-I scores indicates in which extent the product allows the user to identify with it. When evaluated by participants of Group #1, the application scores in these dimensions – 0,8 in HQ-S and 0,9 in HQ-I – indicating that it meets conventional standards in terms of aesthetics and attractiveness, providing users with identification and meeting ordinary standards but with room for further improvements. This is consistent with the qualitative feedback collected through the interviews: as mentioned above, participants referred that some icons were not clear about its function and that their size was too small.

"In my opinion it is a useful application. Nevertheless some graphical (iconographic) improvements are needed" - participant #18

Emotional reactions towards the application were assessed through the SAM-Manikin scale, where scores go from 1 to 9 and are classified as being negative (from 1 to 4), neutral (5) or positive (from 6 to 9). Evaluated by Group #1, the application got a rating of 7,3 on the satisfaction dimension; 6,1 on what concerns motivation; while sense of control was rated as 7,1, indicating that participants felt rather positive effects during the interaction. As for the overall impression of the product, the application score in the Attractiveness dimension (ATT) of AttrakDiff (1,3) indicating that the overall impression of the product is positive (i.e., "very attractive"). This is consistent with the participants' overall opinion, which pointed out the feed area as one of the most important and relevant features/functionalities of the application.

Table 1 resumes the scores attributed to the application by participants of Group #1 in each one of the three considered UX dimensions.

Finally, and questioned if they would use the second-screen application in their daily lives, despite a positive answer from the major part of the sample, 3 out of the 18 participants mentioned that – although considering the application interesting – they would not use it, namely because they were not regular TV consumers.

During the tests, in an overall perspective, no major problems were revealed in terms of navigation (e.g. access to previous markers, access to other features/menu areas); and part of the iconography has been validated.

According to the evaluators feedback, it was possible to identify the following suggestions for improvement: i) to make it clear for the user that he may navigate between markers on the main page (e.g. by including the image of the beginning of the next marker side by side to the main marker); adjust the size and shape of some icons; include additional configuration and personalization settings.

"I just got confused on that feed area. How are the markers sorted?" – participant #3

"I was not seeing (user referring to the Bookmark button) that "ribbon" button... It is too small" – participant #7

This first evaluation was very important in the development of the interface and interaction options. The conclusions from this evaluation were integrated in the following version of the prototype for the final evaluation.

Group #2. As for Group #2, data analysis (see Table 2) shows that when evaluated by the 20 participants the second release of the prototype scored 80,4 (in a maximum of 100) in the SUS scale, and 1 (in a maximum of 3) in the Pragmatic dimension of AttrakDiff. In terms of instrumental qualities, this means that the application has a slightly better level of usability (than on the first release), but still with room for improvement in what concerns its pragmatic qualities. This conclusion was also consistent with the data collected through interviews: when asked to share their opinion regarding the application and its main functionalities, participants characterized it as being "organized", "simple" and "easy to use".

"The navigation seems to be very straightforward" – participant #8

Table 2. Application score according to the SUS, SAM and AttrakDiff instruments (Group #2)

Instrumental qualities	Non-instrumental qualities		Emotional Reactions				
SUS (0 to 100)	AttrakDiff (-3 to 3)		SAM (1 to 9)				AttrakDiff (-3 to 3)
	PQ	HQ-S	HQ-I	Sat.	Mot.	S. of C.	ATT
80,4	1,0	0,4	0,9	7,1	6,0	6,6	1,1

Non-instrumental qualities (closely related with visual aesthetics and identification) were again evaluated through the Hedonic Qualities – Identity (HQ-I) and Stimulation (HQ-S) dimensions – of the AttrakDiff instrument. When evaluated by participants of Group #2, the application scores in these dimensions (0,4 in HQ-S and 0,9 in HQ-I) indicate that it meets conventional standards, providing users with identification and meeting ordinary standards of stimulation but with room for improvements. This is also consistent with the participants' opinions collected during the interviews, where one participant described the application as being "pleasant, with the essential features" (participant #10) and three participants (#3, #12, #15) describe it as being "build according to standards" and "consistent with other Android apps".

Emotional reactions towards the application were at this stage also assessed through the SAM-Manikin scale. Evaluated by Group #2, the application got a rating of 7,1 on the satisfaction dimension; 6 on what concerns motivation; while sense of control was rated as 6,6, indicating that participants felt rather positive effects during the interaction. This score may be a good indicator that, with further developments, the application will have stronger possibilities of being adopted by future users. As for the overall impression of the product, the applications score in the Attractiveness dimension (ATT) of AttrakDiff (1,1) indicates that the overall impression of the product is positive. This is coherent with the participants' opinions collected during the interviews, as 65 % of the participants describe the application as being "organized", and mention that – depending on the TV show they would be watching – they would probably use it in future scenarios.

Table 2 resumes the scores attributed to the application by participants of Group #2 in each one of the three considered UX dimensions.

5   Discussion

By comparing data presented in Tables 1 and 2, it is possible to see that (cf. Table 3) – despite small changes have been made to the applications interface following the results of the first evaluation – the overall opinion about the application has improved in an unbalanced way.

Table 3. Comparison of scores given by Group #1 and Group #2

	Instrumental qualities			Non-instrumental qualities		Emotional Reactions			
	SUS (0 to 100)	AttrakDiff (-3 to 3)					SAM (1 to 9)		AttrakDiff (-3 to 3)
		PQ	HQ-S	HQ-I	Sat.	Mot.	S. of C.		ATT
Group #1	77,1	**1,1**	**0,8**	0,9	**7,3**	**6,1**	**7,1**		**1,3**
Group #2	**80,4**	1,0	0,4	0,9	7,1	6,0	6,6		1,1

With exception of the SUS scores (77,1 for the first session and 80,4 for the second session), AttrakDiff and SAM-Manikin scores slightly decreased from the first to the second evaluation.

Taking into consideration the characteristics of the two groups presented in the "Participants" sub-section, namely in what concerns to Television and Second-screen habits, and despite its small size, it is possible to suggest that having regular habits of using second-screen applications (72 % of participants of Group #1 claimed to use second-screen apps to search for information related with TV shows, while only 25 % of Group #2 claimed the same) may influence the overall impression of other second-screen applications and systems. In a certain extent, this validates Mahlke and Thuring [14] claims that the characteristics of the user, such as knowledge and skills influence the overall experience as much as the characteristics of the system or application (e.g. functionality, interface design).

Moreover, it means that when developing second-screen applications in a UX approach and taking the users' opinions into consideration, developers and designers must work not only towards improving usability but also the whole experience.

This was clearly the case of the context-advertising feature that was introduced just before the second evaluation. The disruptive character of the ads gave the users a sense of not being able to control the application, thus affecting the SAM-Manikin score related with "Sense of Control".

When considered the Control Group, and despite its smaller number of participants, these conclusions can be analyzed in a more meaningful way. When observing Table 4 reflecting the differences in the several analyzed dimensions from the same group of participants involved in the first and second evaluation, it is possible to conclude that as a whole the application has improved in what concerns its usability (SUS), non-instrumental qualities (aesthetics +29 % and identification +14 %) and attractiveness (ATT +18 %). In terms of the dimensions were a decrease was observed, it is important to address the slightly reduction in the Pragmatic Quality (PQ -6 %) that might concern a fortuitous fluctuation of judgment.

Table 4. Comparison of scores given by partipants of the Control Group

	Instrumental qualities			Non-instrumental qualities		Emotional Reactions			
	SUS (0 to 100)	AttrakDiff (-3 to 3)			SAM (1 to 9)			AttrakDiff (-3 to 3)	
		PQ	HQ-S	HQ-I	Sat.	Mot.	S. of C.	ATT	
CG fore	73,6	**0,95**	0,5	0,6	6,7	**6,2**	**7,8**	0,9	
CG after	**80,6**	0,9	**0,7**	**0,7**	6,7	5,6	6,9	**1,1**	

The more relevant drop in the remaining two dimensions of the SAM-Manikin scores (Motivation -11 % and Sense of Control -13 %) might be explained with the difference of results on some of the Attrakdiff "pairs of words". As an example, it is possible to observe a significant inversion (from the first to the second evaluation) on the classification of the set "unpredictable" versus "predictable" probably due to the referred approach to present users with unexpected ads.

6 Conclusions

The growing adoption of mobile devices as additional platforms for watching video and television content fostered the development of services and applications designed to deliver additional information related with the TV content. Mobile devices, however, have specificities that create multiple challenges in the field of User Experience, emphasizing the need, when developing second-screen applications, to consider dimensions such as the emotional impact and user's engagement with the product.

In this paper, authors introduced the development process of a second-screen application able to automatically identify content being displayed on the television screen and present related synchronized information. As the development was conducted under a UX participatory approach, users' opinions were considered in all stages of the process, aiming for a better, more intuitive, engaging and ease to use application. By including users in early stages of the development process and by asking them to evaluate the application instrumental and non-instrumental qualities and considering their emotional reactions it was possible to estimate not only the application usability but also its impact and ability to motivate and create better user experiences.

The adopted UX evaluation was supported in a common ground procedure in what relates to considering a control group and a script suitable to evaluate non work-oriented applications (balancing free and guided usage of the application). In addition, a qualitative gathering of data (through interviews and a think aloud protocol) combined with validated instruments as proved to be an efficient approach. Actually, the triangulation of the SAM, SUS and Attrakdiff questionnaires (presented to the participants in this order) allowed to extract important and consistent conclusions in what relates to the Instrumental Qualities of the application being evaluated (obtained from a combination of the SUS and Attrakdiff - PQ dimension); its Non-instrumental Qualities (from HQ-S and HQ-I dimensions of Attrakdiff); and Emotional Reactions (obtained through SAM and ATT dimension of Attrakdiff).

Acknowledgements. This paper is a result of the 2NDVISION project, funded by QREN (grant agreement no. 38783). Authors are grateful to Mónica Aresta, Lígia Duro, Rita Oliveira and André Ferreira for their work on the project and also to the remaining project partners: Altran and Outsoft.

References

1. Jancovich, M.: Time, scheduling and cinema-going. Media International Australia. Incorporating Culture Policy, no. 139, pp. 88–95 (2011). http://search.informit.com.au/documentSummary;dn=055670613543388;res=IELLCC, ISSN: 1329-878X

2. Abreu, J., Almeida, P., Teles, B., Reis, M.: Viewer behaviors and practices in the (new) television environment. In: Proceedings of the 11th European Conference on Interactive TV and Video (EuroITV 2013), pp. 5–12. ACM, New York (2013). http://dx.doi.org/10.1145/2465958.2465970
3. Geerts, D., Leenheer, D., Heijstraten, S., Negenman, J.: In front of and behind the second screen: viewer and producer perspectives on a companion App. In: Proceedings of the TVX 2014 Conference, 25–27 June 2014, Newcastle Upon Tyne, UK, pp. 95–102 (2014)
4. Sun, X., May, M.: Design of the user experience for personalized mobile services. Int. J. Hum. Comput. Interact. (IJHCI) **5**(2), 21–39 (2014)
5. Solano, A., Collazos, C., Rusu, C., Merchan, L.: Evaluating the usability of interactive digital television Applications. In: 2013 Tenth International Conference on Information Technology: New Generations (ITNG), pp. 127–132. IEEE, April 2013
6. The Nielsen Company: Screen wars: the battle for eye space in a TV-everywhere world, March 2015. http://www.nielsen.com/us/en/insights/reports/2015/screen-wars-the-battle-for-eye-space-in-a-tv-everywhere-world.html. Accessed 13 June 2015
7. Red Bee Media: Second Screen Series - Paper 1: Setting The Scene (2012). http://www.redbeemedia.com/sites/all/files/downloads/second_screen_series_paper_1_whitepaper_red_bee_media.pdf
8. Cano, P., Batle, E., Kalker, T., Haitsma, J.: A review of algorithms for audio fingerprinting. In: Paper Presented at the 2002 IEEE Workshop on Multimedia Signal Processing (2002)
9. ISO DIS 9241-210:2010: Ergonomics of human system interaction -Part 210: Human-centred design for interactive systems (formerly known as 13407). International Standardization Organization (ISO), Switzerland
10. Zhang, D., Adipat, B.: Challenges, methodologies, and issues in the usability testing of mobile applications. Int. J. Hum. Comput. Interact. **18**(3), 293–308 (2005). doi:10.1207/s15327590ijhc1803_3
11. Treder, M., Pachucki, A., Zielonko, A., Łukasiewicz, K.: Mobile book of trends 2014. UX Pin & Movade internal report (2014). http://studio.uxpin.com/ebooks/mobile-design-book-of-trends/
12. Bank, C., Zuberi, W.: Mobile UI design patterns. UX Pin & Movade internal report (2014). http://studio.uxpin.com/ebooks/mobile-design-patterns/
13. Lee, K., Flinn, J., Giuli, T., Noble, B., Peplin, C.: AMC: verifying user interface properties for vehicular applications. In: MobiSys 2013, 25–28 June 2013, Taipei, Taiwan (2013)
14. Mahlke, S., Thuring, M.: Studying antecedents of emotional experiences in interactive contexts. In: CHI 2007 Proceedings - Emotion & Empathy. San Jose, CA (2007)
15. Gross, A., Bongartz, S.: Why do I like it? Investigating the product-specificity of user experience. In: Proceedings of the 7th Nordic Conference on Human-Computer Interaction: Making Sense Through Design (NordiCHI 2012), pp. 322–330. ACM, New York (2012). http://dx.doi.org/10.1145/2399016.2399067
16. Law, E., Schaik, P., Roto, V.: Attitudes towards user experience (UX) measurement. Int. J. Hum Comput Stud. **72**(6), 526–541 (2014). http://dx.doi.org/10.1016/j.ijhcs.2013.09.006, ISSN 1071-5819
17. Bach, C., Gauducheau, N., Salembier, P.: Combining interviews and scales in the multidimensional evaluation of user experience: a case study in 3D games. In: Proceedings of the 29th Annual European Conference on Cognitive Ergonomics (ECCE 2011), pp. 157–160. ACM, New York (2011). http://dx.doi.org/10.1145/2074712.2074743
18. Aranyi, G., van Schaik, P.: Modeling user-experience with news Web sites. J. Assoc. Inf. Sci. Technol. **66**, 1–23 (2014). http://onlinelibrary.wiley.com/doi/10.1002/asi.23348/epdf

19. Brooke, J.: SUS-A quick and dirty usability scale. In: Jordan, P.W., Weerdmeester, P.W., Thomas, P.W., McLelland, I.L. (eds.) Usability Evaluation in Industry, pp. 189–194. Taylor and Francis, London (1996)
20. Attrakdiff (2011). http://www.attrakdiff.de/
21. Bernhaupt, R., Pirker, M.: Evaluating user experience for interactive television: towards the development of a domain-specific user experience questionnaire. In: Kotzé, P., Marsden, G., Lindgaard, G., Wesson, J., Winckler, M. (eds.) INTERACT 2013, Part II. LNCS, vol. 8118, pp. 642–659. Springer, Heidelberg (2013)
22. Bradley, M.M., Lang, P.J.: Measuring emotion: the self-assessment manikin and the semantic differential. J. Behav. Ther. Exper. Psychiatry $25(1)$, 49–59 (1994)
23. Bangor, A., Kortum, P.T., Miller, J.T.: An empirical evaluation of the system usability scale. Int. J. Hum. Comput. Interact. $24(6)$, 574–594 (2008)

News Reports on TV, Twitter and the Active Audience

Luis E. Martinez-Martínez[1(✉)] and Laura Martínez-Espinosa[2(✉)]

[1] Alicante University, Alicante, Spain
tascaband@gmail.com
[2] Cardenal Herrera CEU University, Valencia, Spain
lauramartinezespinosa@gmail.com

Abstract. Twitter has established itself as one of the most influential social networks. This article performs a content analysis on the five Twitter profiles of the five news programs broadcast by general-interest TV networks in Spain according to the audience ranking provided by Kantar Media.

We have defined variables that include the description of the news profiles, type of post, frequency, response and user interaction, analysing the capacity of news programs to use Twitter to disseminate content and generate conversation, their acquired reputation, and user quality.

Keywords: Journalism · Communication · Internet · Social media · Twitter · Digital media · Interactivity · Second screen · Interactive television

1 Introduction

Television is still the leading media in society, with a penetration of 88.3 % according to 2014 data from AIMC [1] and Kantar Media [2]. Despite having less penetration than television, Internet has been experiencing slight growth in recent years. Accordingly, Internet is the medium where the greatest increases in daily users and interaction are being noted. This is proved by EGM [3] figures for 2015. In 2013, 25.379 % of the population used Internet; in 2014 this figure increased to 27.015 % and in 2015 it increased further to 29.103 %.

Audiovisual is the king of the media. Television has evolved, becoming more alive than ever, as some authors have noted. We are dealing with a new medium, one whose content invades Internet. We may therefore say that television offers a new way of interacting with users, via Internet and, by extension, the social networks.

According to Castells [4], television is increasingly approaching the social media, interacting with users and creating constant feedback. While it is true that the social media have the news before television, this is also the space where the networks have their social profiles, apps and digital television.

A study published by eMarketer in 2014 [5] showed that half of all adults in North America checked their social media profiles while they watched TV and that one out of six commented on what they were watching.

According to a 2012 study by Nielsen [6], Twitter influences dozens of television programs. According to this analysis, "reality shows" had the strongest influence (44 %),

© Springer International Publishing Switzerland 2016
M.J. Abásolo et al. (Eds.): jAUTI 2015/CTVDI 2015, CCIS 605, pp. 121–133, 2016.
DOI: 10.1007/978-3-319-38907-3_10

followed by comedy shows (37 %). The most striking figures came from sporting events and monthly television programming, which generated 50 % of all social activity developed around TV.

The media increasingly rely on Internet, using it as a tool to improve and increase participation.

The media have discovered in the social media an additional means of connecting with audiences. One of the social networks experiencing the greatest growth is Twitter, the micro-blogging platform that allows users or subscribers to post brief comments about their activities.

Although society still prefers TV for breaking news, Twitter proved to be an important source for the immediate transmission of information.

Social networks have changed the way we consume TV and platforms such as Twitter have become undisputed stars of TV. Indeed, according to the study, 95 % of online conversations about TV take place on Twitter [5].

Researchers from Carnegie Mellon University in the United States performed a textual analysis of Twitter posts and found that the it may be used as a means to assess public opinion [7].

With regard to the Internet sites most visited by users, social media occupy the fourth place on the list. Facebook is the undisputed leader of the social media, with 96 % growth and penetration, followed by YouTube (66 %) and Twitter (56 %). A study on social networks performed by IAB Spain [8] shows that Youtube continues to be the most highly-valued social network, followed by Spotify, Instagram and Facebook, while the least valued are Tuenti, Badoo and Google+.

Twitter is the social network that has most grown over recent years, occupying the fifth spot in the ranking of best networks.

With regard to frequency of usage, the study shows that average use is 3.6 days per week, Facebook once again featuring as the network with the highest frequency of use (every day), followed by Twitter. Instagram follows closely behind Twitter in third place, overtaking the Youtube video network.

Twitter allows all users to participate directly in the development of news messages, in what the authors call 'participatory journalism'. This is possible thanks to the built-in interactivity and referential ability provided by Twitter [9].

The media need to promote their strategies in the social networks, exploring the possibility of attracting new interest groups as audience. We are dealing now with journalism 2.0, "a new, comprehensive and totally different journalistic style: in the matters they address, in their treatment of the reader, and in providing references, links and hypertext, as well as their instantaneity, etc." [10].

At this stage, we are taking about journalism 3.0, the term coined by Dan Gillmor to refer to information made digital by the media. The audience participates in the creation of the news. Posting the article on the social media is not the end of the process, as readers comment, debate and share content, at times generating a fluid digital conversation. Up till now, with traditional media, this was not possible [10].

The main use of the social networks continues to be social, and the favourite activities of the users continue to include checking what their contacts are doing (66 %), videos and music (58 %), sending messages (52 %), publishing content (39 %) and chatting (37 %).

The novelty is commenting on current affairs, an activity that has risen since last year, achieving 34 % penetration. This figure is linked to the sectors most followed by the social media: telecommunications and technology (39 %) and culture and media (37 %).

Also interesting is the age of the users who access social media. Facebook, Youtube and Twitter, the most popular platforms, have similar sets of followers. In the case of persons who have access to Facebook, 78 % are aged 14–17 years, and 96 % are aged 18–55 years.

In the case of Youtube, 70 % are aged 14–17 years, while 66 % are aged 18 to 55 years. Lastly, Twitter reaches 61 % in the first range and 56 % in the second.

The social media are places on the internet where users can connect with other users to create a personal or professional network. One of the main objectives of social media is activity, encouraging users to participate or to increase their participation.

Twitter is a powerful communications tool. "It allows any company to open a bidirectional, interactive communication channel with customers, suppliers, readers and employees" [11]. Dorsey [12], the creator of Twitter explains, "With Twitter, we are in daily contact, we know what we're all doing without having to talk on the phone, people are less inhibited, it's a way of being more united, of sharing more stuff." Cobos [13], on the other hand, defines Twitter as "a way for users to relate with their followers, publishing posts, known as tweets", read by hundreds of people daily.

Cortes [14] defines the social network as "inviting users to publish entries with the question 'What are doing?'". Thanks to its simplicity and constant evolution; Twitter has gone from being "a communication platform to being an almost indispensable tool in some environments."

On the other hand, "DigitalNewsReport.es 2015" [15], drawn up by the Department of Communications at the University of Navarra, maintains that the social networks are the best platform on which to discover news and content (20 %), but that television, which has a larger audience, continues to be the leader among Internet users for confidence, accuracy and reliability, analysis and opinion, and speed of coverage. Twitter and YouTube tie in third position as social media for consumption, dissemination and interaction with news (22 %). In terms of consumption of video news, 27 % of users consume online news videos throughout the week, a 10 % increase over 2014; 23 % check out photo galleries.

This report reveals that what Internet users seek when the consume news is emerging news and context, rather than entertainment. "80 % of Internet users get their news through the social networks because they want to know what is happening in the world around them, and 78 % are interested in understanding the issues that may affect them."

With regard to television, the latest data on the behaviour of television audiences, from April 2015, show that Telecinco (14.8 %) was the leading network for the eighth straight month. According to the latest report from Kantar Media, Telecinco news programs are the most viewed, with the audience weighted for the midday and evening issues, while Antena 3 is leader in the afternoon segment from Monday to Sunday.

With new technologies, the traditional media are incorporating new audience participation and conversation channels, or at least that should be their aim. Viewers are no longer mere consumers of information, but active users of a service with which they decide to interact. With regard to journalists, their generally active participation in

Twitter is evident, although this may often entail the dangers of unlimited first-hand access to information [16, 17].

2   Material and Methods

The main aim of this study is to analyse the Twitter presence and use of the five most influential general-interest TV networks in Spain over 1 to 30 June 2015, as well as the results of their Twitter use.

The methodology used in this study is "a systematic, controlled, empirical, non-judgemental, public investigation, critical of natural phenomena. It is guided by theory and hypotheses regarding the alleged relations between phenomena" [18].

Content analysis was used, this being the ideal tool for studying Twitter content. According to Bardin [19], we chose this technique since as it is ideal for the aims of this study. Also according to other authors, including Castello and Ramos [20], the content analysis method makes systematic, objective and quantitative study of Twitter communication possible, measuring certain variables.

This article performs a content analysis on the Twitter profiles of the five leading news programs broadcast by general-interest TV networks in Spain, according to the audience ranking provided by Kantar Media. In this study, we have defined valuables for each network, including number of followers and profiles followed, average number of tweets per day, number of tweets in which the user mentions the network, number of links contained in each tweet, total number of tweets, number of tweets that are retweets, tweets retweeted by others, tweets favourited by others, hashtag use, number of tweets per day of the week by each network and number of tweets by time of day, in hourly segments. Analysing these data provides us with information including the description of the news profiles, type of publication, frequency, response and user interaction, analysing the capacity of the news programs to use Twitter to disseminate content and generate conversation, their acquired reputation, and the quality of their users.

The data were analysed using the Tweetchup free tool, one that is surprisingly easy to use and gives access to key statistical information.

To choose the sample, this study took into account the ranking of television media and general-interest network news programs drawn up in April 2015 by Barlovento Comunicación, using data from Kantar Media, the most popular being Telecinco, Antena 3, Televisión Española and La Sexta (ahead of Cuatro by 234,000 spectators).

The news programs of the leading networks are re-broadcast on Twitter, by means of Tweets which, in turn, may include links to photos or video. By means of this new strategy, news networks can interact with viewers, allowing them to participate in and be involved in the story.

As mentioned already, Twitter is growing daily with regard to the set of variables to be taken into account. These include: number of tweeps (coverage), number of users, level of conversation, activity, hashtags, favourites, tweets, retweets, engagement, quality of followers, etc. In order to correctly understand the variables analysed in this study, we considered defining each of the terms using Twitonomy, the Marketing and Social Media dictionary published by the PuroMarketing [21].

Hashtag: Twitter labels. Used basically to generate discussion on a particular topic. A hash symbol is placed before the keyword (e.g.,#marketing).

Tweet: short (140-character maximum) public messages posted on Twitter.

Followers: number of followers.

Following: number of users followed by the network.

Retweets: number of times a tweet is re-posted.

Favourite: number of times a tweet is marked as favourite.

Quality of followers: based on influence, interaction and number of followers.

Tweets per day: average number of tweets posted each day. The higher this number, the more active the Twitter user is.

Links: average number of links on Twitter. The greater the number of links, the more likely it is that the user is a source of information on Twitter.

Mentions: proportion of mentions that are direct responses to tweets.

Engagement: generating an emotional bond between brand and consumer.

From the point of view of the media, Twitter appears to be well accepted, because it allows headlines to be sent. The leading networks personalise their messages, seeking proximity and empathy, using colloquial language and second person pronouns to engage with users.

We have taken the following hypotheses into account in this study:

H1: Increased activity (average number of tweets per day) by news media is linked to increased follower numbers.

H2: The number of people followed by each Twitter profile is greater than the number of followers.

H3: There is a link between the number of tweets per hour and the time the news program is broadcast.

H4: There is a link between the number of tweets containing links and the number of mentions.

H5: News programs generally use hashtags to generate debate among viewers.

H6: The network with the most viewers, Telecinco, gets more retweets than the other networks.

H7: News program feedback on Twitter is bidirectional, with a high percentage of messages being favourited by users.

H8: There is a working structure which includes a number of Tweets per day.

3   Results

As Table 1 shows, the highest number of followers is held by @A3Noticias, with 931,294, followed by @SextaNoticias and @Noticias_cuatro. It is striking that @tele-diario_tve is the last in follower numbers.

Table 1. Followers of each network on Twitter

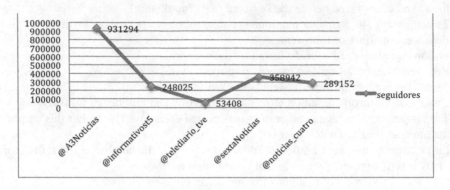

Table 2. Number of users followed by each network

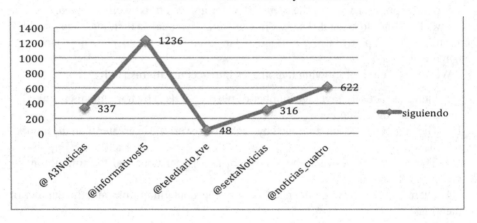

Table 3. Average number of tweets per day

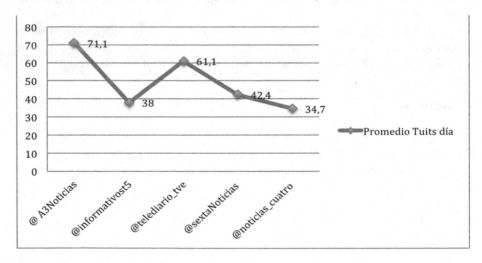

Table 2 shows that @Informativost5 is the network that follows most users, followed by @noticias_cuatro; once again, @telediario_tve brings up the rear, following only 48 users.

Table 3 indicates that the highest average of Tweets is by @A3Noticias, followed by @telediario_tve and @sextaNoticias, with @noticias_cuatro in last place.

As Table 4 shows, the best result for users mentioning the network in their tweets is for @sextaNoticias, followed by @telediario_tve, with @informativost5 in last place.

Table 4. User mentions in tweets

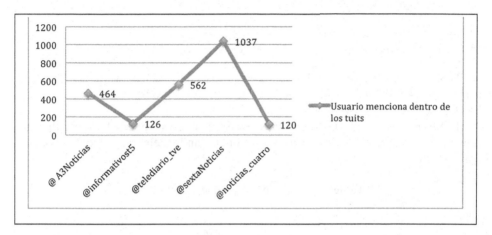

In Table 5, number of Tweets containing links posted by the networks, @A3Noticias leads the way, followed by @telediario_tve and @SextaNoticias, with @Informativost5 and @noticias_cuatro in last place.

Table 5. Links within tweets

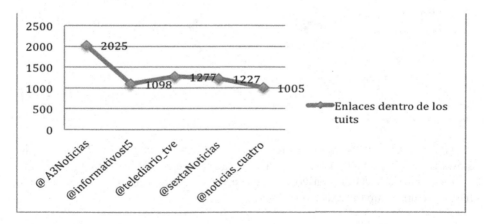

Table 6. Total tweets per network

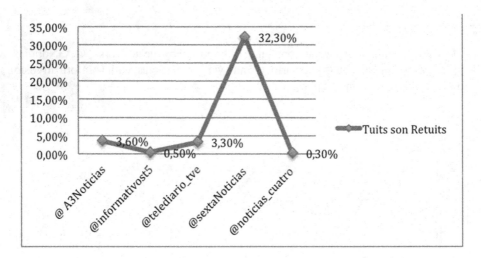

Table 6 shows the total number of tweets published by each network. @A3Noticias is at the head, followed by @sextanoticias. @noticias_cuatro brings up the rear, with a level of activity far below the average.

Table 7 shows that @sextanoticias leads easily in number of tweets that are retweets, with 32.3 %, followed by @A3Noticias and @telediario_tve, both a long way behind.

Table 7. Number of tweets that are retweeted

The number of network tweets retweeted by others is contained in Table 8, which shows that 99.9 % of @SextaNoticias tweets are retweeted, followed by @A3Noticias with 99.1 %, then @Informativost5 and @noticias_cuatro with 95.2 % each; @tele-diario_tve brings up the rear with 88.3 %.

Table 8. Tweets retweeted by others

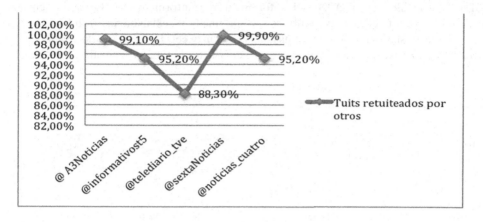

Table 9. Tweets favourited by others

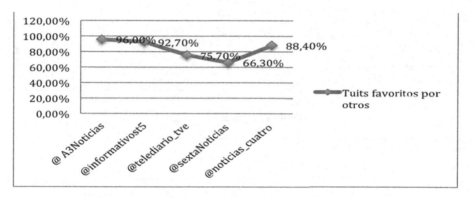

Table 10. Number of hashtags used

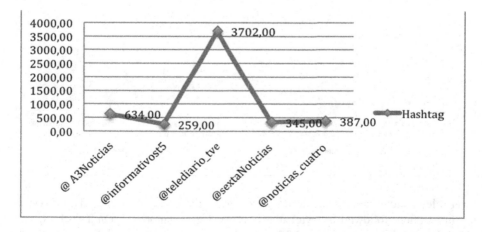

The favorites section is very tight (Table 9), falling within a range of 66 %–96 %. The best result is for @A3Noticias, followed by @informativost5, @noticias_cuatro with 88.4 %, @telediario_tve with 75.7 % and finally @sextaNoticias with 66.3 %.

Table 10 shows the number of hashtags used in tweets by the networks examined in this study. As we can see, @telediario_tve clearly uses more hashtags than the others.

Table 11. Number of Tweets per day

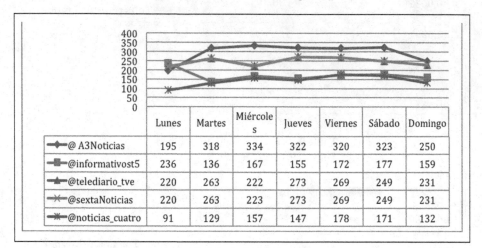

	Lunes	Martes	Miércoles	Jueves	Viernes	Sábado	Domingo
@ A3Noticias	195	318	334	322	320	323	250
@informativost5	236	136	167	155	172	177	159
@telediario_tve	220	263	222	273	269	249	231
@sextaNoticias	220	263	223	273	269	249	231
@noticias_cuatro	91	129	157	147	178	171	132

Table 12. Tweets per hour

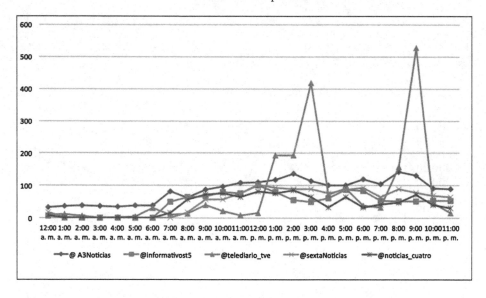

Table 11 shows the number of tweets per day. On Mondays, @informativost5 tweets the most often, followed by @telediario_tve and @sextanoticias. On Tuesdays, first place is held by @A3Noticias, followed by @telediario_tve and @sextaNoticias.

Wednesdays are led by @A3Noticias, followed by @SextaNoticias and @tele-diario_tve. Thursdays are also led by @A3Noticias, followed by @SextaNoticias and @telediario_tve; these top three places are maintained through to the end of the week.

Table 12 indicates very clearly that the leader in temporary tweet location is @tele-diario_tve, at a considerable distance from the other news programs, even at the times the programs are broadcast. These times are different from those of @telediario_tve, which reaches a high point from 1:00 p.m. to 3:00 p.m. and peaks at 9:00 p.m

4   Conclusions and Notes

Throughout this study we analysed the Twitter profiles of the five news programs with most viewers included on the ranking of television media and general-interest network news programs for April 2015 drawn up by Barlovento Comunicación using data from Kantar Media [22].

Using the Tweetchup free tool, we analysed how TV news programs use Twitter, examining their profiles, their impact, and audience behaviour.

Our findings will be used to draw up a detailed inventory of the use of each profile on the platform, as well as giving an overview of the trends followed by the sample. We also offer an understanding of the possible relationships between the variables analysed.

Following an empirical process, a series of hypotheses were raised, to be then confirmed or refuted.

With regard to the first hypothesis: "Increased activity (tweets total) by news programs is linked to a higher number of followers". Table 6 shows that @A3Noticias is in the lead, followed by @sextanoticias, with @informativost5 in third place, @tele-diario_tve in fourth place and @Noticias_cuatro bringing up the rear. In Table 1, the first position is held by @A3Noticias, followed by @SextaNoticias, with @Noti-cias_cuatro in third place, followed by @informativost5 and finally @telediario_tve. Accordingly, this hypothesis must be refuted as, although @A3Noticias and @sexta-noticias may seem to indicate a link, this is not reliably followed in the other three cases.

Second hypothesis: "The number of people followed by each profile is greater than the number of followers". Having analysed Tables 1 and 2 we must refute the hypothesis, as the number of followers is higher than the number of people followed. We should note that it seems appropriate that any media with a social media profile should aim at symmetrical two-way communication (Grünig, 2003), [23] allowing bidirectionality between news and the audience. On the other hand, interactivity and two-way commu-nication between audience and news program may favour audience participation in the new communicative framework. This model also makes it easier to know the audience, understand their needs, ensure the sale of the news product, maintain user loyalty and increase the social influence of the program. (Salaverría, 2005). [24].

Third hypothesis: "There is a link between the number of Tweets per hour and the time the news program is broadcast." Having examined Table 12 and taking into account the time each program is broadcast, we must confirm this hypothesis, as there is a notable increase in the number of tweets while each program is being broadcast.

Fourth hypothesis: "There is a link between the number of Tweets containing links and the number of mentions." In accordance with the Tables 4 and 5, we must conclude that there is no link between the number of tweets containing links and the number of mentions; accordingly, we must refute this hypothesis.

Fifth hypothesis: "News programs generally use hashtags to generate debate among viewers." Looking at Table 10, we observe that @telediario_tve makes the most use of hashtags to generate debate among viewers, but this rule is not followed so closely by the other networks. Accordingly, we must refute this hypothesis. We should mention the increase in hashtag use by most TV programs, both to generate debate and as a tool to study and analyse the scope and impact of each news item, favouring the decision-making process.

Sixth hypothesis: "The network with the most viewers, Telecinco, gets more retweets than the other networks." A look at Table 8 shows that @informativost5 is not the profile that receives the most retweets, even though it has the largest TV audience. Accordingly, the Sixth hypothesis must be rejected.

Seventh hypothesis: "News program feedback on Twitter is bidirectional, with a high percentage of messages being favourited by users." Having examined Table 9, we see that the favourites section is very homogenous - from 66 % to 96 %. We may conclude that there is a high percentage of user favorites, which would indicate bidirectionality. Therefore, we may confirm this hypothesis.

Eighth hypothesis: "There is a working structure which includes a number of tweets per day". If we look at Table 11, we see a certain uniformity in the number of tweets published every day of the week by each profile, so we can confirm this hypothesis.

As a general note and for future research, it would be interesting to expand the research, analysing viewer profiles and including psychological and social variables, affinities and visual and auditory preferences, for a better understanding of the possible link between decision-making and Twitter use.

References

1. AIMC: Navegantes en la Red (2012). http://www.aimc.es/-Navegantes-en-la-Red-.html. (Citation date: 12 Jan 2015)
2. Kantar Media & Barlovento Comunicación. El Comportamiento de la Audiencia Televisiva: May 2015 (2015). (Citation date: 12 Jan 2015)
3. EGM, Audiencia en Internet Febrero–Marzo (2015). http://www.aimc.es/-Audiencia-de-Internet-en-el-EGM-.html. (Citation date: 12 Jan 2015)
4. Castells, M. Internet y la sociedad red. La factoría (2001)
5. Emarketer. http://www.emarketer.com/Article/Global-Ad-Spending-Growth-Double-This-Year/1010997. (Citation date: 12 Jan 2015)
6. Nielsen, State of The Media–The Social Media Report (2012). (April 2014)
7. O'Connor, B., Routledge, S.: La medición del desempeño social empresarial a través de las redes sociales. Contaduría y Administración **59**(2), 121–143 (2010). Apr–June, 2014
8. IAB. VI Estudio Redes Sociales de IAB Spain (2015). http://www.iabspain.net/wp-content/uploads/downloads/2015/01/Estudio_Anual_Redes_Sociales_2015.pdf
9. Bowman, S., Willis, C.: The future is here, but do news media companies see it? Nieman Rep. **59**(4), 6–10 (2005)

10. Montoya, P.G.A.: Periodismo digital y periodismo ciudadano. Análisis y propuestas en torno al periodismo digital: VII Congreso Nacional Periodismo Digital, 2 y 3 de marzo de 2006, Huesca, pp. 251–262. Aragón Press Association (2006)
11. Liberos, E.: El libro del marketing interactivo y la publicidad digital. ESIC Editorial, España (2013)
12. Dorsey, J. Entrevista a Jack Dorsey (2010). http://egkafati.bligoo.com/content/view/877481/entrevista-a-jack-dorsey.html#.VCh6ril_sdQ. (Citation date: 22 Aug 2015)
13. Cobos, T.L.: Twitter como fuente para periodistas latinoamericanos. Razón y Palabra **15**(73), 1–35 (2010)
14. Cortés, M.: Nanoblogging: los usos de las nuevas plataformas de comunicación en la red. UOC (2009)
15. DigitalNewsReport.es (2015). http://www.digitalnewsreport.es/. (Citation date 15 Jan 2015)
16. Souter, J.: "Is social media the journalism of the future?" Daily Record (2009)
17. Safko, L.: The Social Media Bible: Tactics, Tools, and Strategies for Business Success. Wiley, New Jersey (2010)
18. Kerlinger, F.N., Lee, H.B.: Investigación del comportamiento: métodos de investigación en ciencias sociales. McGraw-Hill, Mexico (2001)
19. Bardin, L.: El análisis de contenido. Akal, Madrid (1986)
20. Castelló, A.: El uso de hashtags en Twitter por parte de los programas de televisión españoles (2013). http://reunir.unir.net/handle/123456789/1762. (Citation date, 11 Sept 2015)
21. Diccionario de Marketing y Social Media, Revista PuroMarketing. http://www.puromarketing.com/diccionario-marketing. (Fecha de consulta: 12 Jan 2015)
22. Kantar Media & Barlovento Comunicación. El Comportamiento de la Audiencia Televisiva: Mayo (2015). http://www.barloventocomunicacion.es/images/publicaciones/barlovento-audiencias-mayo-2015.pdf
23. Grunig, J.E., Dozier, D.M.: Excellent public relations and effective organizations: a study of communication management in three countries. Routledge (2003)
24. Salaverría, R.: Cibermedios: el impacto de Internet en los medios de comunicación en España, vol. 15. Comunicación Social, Sevilla (2005)

Approach to a Pedagogical Model of iDTV. Methodology for the Analysis of Interactions

Andrea Miranda$^{(\boxtimes)}$, Graciela Santos, and Silvia Stipcich

ECienTec, Facultad de Ciencias Exactas, UNICEN, Tandil, Argentina
{amiranda,nsantos,sstipcich}@exa.unicen.edu.ar

Abstract. Activities promoting dialogic interactions between user and application are based on technology-enhanced pedagogical models that focus on the potential of the applications.

This work presents a methodological approach to analyze the digital narrative that a person develops in association with the interactive iDTV application. The methodology consists of recording the user′s actions to recreate interaction narratives. The aim is to identify actions that modify the development of the activity and generate changes in the way the user approaches the object. According to these actions (disturbances) data are fragmented into a set of interaction segments based on which each viewer′s work style is inferred.

The reconstruction of digital narrative provides information about the interactive processes to develop more elaborate pedagogical models.

Keywords: Digital interaction · Educational content · iDTV

1 Introduction

The technological advances in iDTV have brought about a communication paradigm shift. Interaction has changed the role of passive viewers involved in one-way communication, and turned them into active users who manage the content.

Interaction and digitization provide the main features of the iDTV content. Digitization makes it possible to include quality images and sound [1], as well as to edit and reuse the multimedia content. Interactivity determines the digital media and enables the user to change the flow and shape of the content. That is, it allows the user to interact with the medium developing in this way the "digital narrative".

Interaction promotes personal learning strategies [2] that allow users to create narratives that suit their interests. The user manages the virtual objects (texts, images, sounds, etc.) to obtain the desired result, and generates different system states at each stage of the process. The user takes now an active role, and performs dialogic actions with the content [3].

Interactions take place in the space where the application interface and the rest of the elements blend together. Such interactions involve social, cognitive and digital dimensions. It should be noted that complex cognitive and semiotic processes lie behind the apparent transparency and automaticity of the interaction [4].

The process of designing and developing educational content for iDTV is a very complex one and combines computer interactivity with traditional TV educational

© Springer International Publishing Switzerland 2016
M.J. Abásolo et al. (Eds.): jAUTI 2015/CTVDI 2015, CCIS 605, pp. 134–146, 2016.
DOI: 10.1007/978-3-319-38907-3_11

models. The characteristics of the designs are similar to those of the instructional models used in e-learning to provide flexible and personalized education [5].

Interactivity offers options to produce adaptable and entertaining educational content for iDTV, with the potential to attract viewers' attention and turn them into active learners. The challenge is to develop pedagogical models that facilitate learning for a diverse audience varying in age and educational level. According to Abadía [6], there is a lack of studies that explain how to integrate the way in which people learn into this kind of environment.

This work is the first stage of a research project aimed at studying the relationship between interaction and pedagogical model in the production of content and learning processes in an iDTV-based environment. This article presents a methodological approach for the analysis of digital narratives that a person develops in association with the interactive iDTV application.

The aim is to reconstruct the digital narratives according to what the person says and does and on the feedback from the application. An ad hoc interactive content was created to assess of the interactions, in order to identify the characteristics that a pedagogical model for iDTV should have.

Section 2 below outlines the pedagogical aspects involved in the design of interactive content. Section 3 deals with the process of "ad hoc" interactive content design. Section 4 presents the methodology for the reconstruction and analysis of interactive processes. Finally, Sect. 5 presents a summary of the results obtained and discusses the implications for the redesign of interactive content.

2 Pedagogical Frame

Technology-enhanced pedagogical models take into account the potential of the applications used for learning activities that promote dialogic interactions between the learner and the application. This dialogue is built around the user's declarative and procedural knowledge, the representations enabled by the different activity system devices [7], and the construction of new knowledge.

The constructivist paradigm assumes that students are actively involved in learning and take control of the process. In this regard, the activity is crucial and should present a challenge to promote critical thinking. For example, it may be a question, problem or situation.

In most activities, learning ones in particular, there are support systems for cognition, which are oriented towards existing *knowledge*; *representations,* or ways of symbolizing knowledge; *retrieval,* or ways of finding knowledge; and *reconstruction,* or new ways of structuring knowledge [8]. These notions guide the study of mediated learning interactions.

To study interactions in technological contexts, a cognitive and interpretative approach can be used. Such approach regards the interface as a text with which the user interacts to achieve a particular objective [4]. The text is built during the interaction and a particular narrative is generated for each situation. According to the instrumental genesis approach [9], in the user's narrative is reflected the integration of the artifacts in the activity. They are processes of accommodation and assimilation by which the person appropriates the device and gives it meaning as an instrument.

The content for iDTV may adopt an instructional, constructivist or recreational approach [10]. In either case, the pedagogical intention should determine the content, in direct relation with the interaction.

3   iDTV Content Design and Implementation

The relationship between a device and its use is a complex one. According to Rabardel and Bourmaud [11], the design of an artifact is a process that continues when it is used. These authors take an instrumental approach centered around the integration of the artifact into the structure of human activities [12]. They argue that a person activates appropriation processes when using an artifact to perform an activity—by refining the artifact utilization schemes (those included in its design), the personal ones (those developed when interacting with other artifact), and the ad hoc ones (those the person creates to do specific activities for which the artifact has not been designed).

That is, a user-centered perspective is adopted. The focus shifts from the application to what the user is most capable of doing with it. The authors take into account the dual nature of instruments: that which comes from the artifact itself, and that which originates with the user's utilization schemes [11].

The instrumental meaning given to the artefact depends on the activity, specific conditions, existing knowledge, needs, etc. The interaction has learning characteristics and allows the user to gain more expertise.

A pedagogical model that provides the answers to application design questions— what, what for, when, and how—should consider the particularities of the associated content. Non-interactive content may be aimed at providing information, or, in the case of telling a story, at making the viewer reflect on the situation presented. In other words, interaction will take place depending on the knowledge available—the user is not encouraged to perform an action on the application and redirect his thought according to the response. The aim of some interactive content may be to provide information requested by the viewer just like an internet search; the viewer may be interested in some particular information or may simply view the information the application offers. In the second case, the viewer has a passive role and does not use the available interactivity. The difference between interactive content and that of traditional TV lies in the fact that the viewer has the control. To sum up, interactivity promotes an action on the part of the user, which results in an identifiable record of an exchange between viewer and content.

To illustrate the analysis of digital narratives, ad hoc content was designed and implemented, using some linear educational content available on YouTube. This video (Fig. 1) was produced by students from the Faculty of Arts of Universidad Nacional del Centro de la Provincia de Buenos Aires for PuntoVerde Tandil, and deals with the subject of environmental care [13]. The animation explores the issue of the plastic used in bags and bottles.

Interactive content requires a non-linear production format. In this case, the original content was divided into several video segments that revolve around four concepts: a

Fig. 1. Video without interactivity became hyper content [13]

main concept (the use of plastic bags) and three secondary ones (decomposition time of plastic, effects on the environment, and garbage). The part of the film that introduces the problem and presents the concepts was regarded as the content backbone and then hyperlinks were created at specific points.

By combining "texts" in different formats—audio, video, images, and written text—hyper-content was therefore produced, which consisted of a main script with entry points to interactive complements that also have their own scripts [14] that develop the secondary concepts.

Figure 2 shows the relationship among the multimedia objects in relation to a timeline. The objects are displayed for an explicit period of time relative to the main video and interactivity is enabled on one of the objects for a given time interval. By

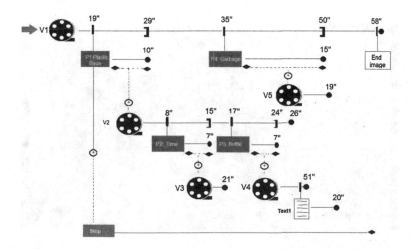

Fig. 2. Timeline of the iDTV interactive content, model adapted from [15]

clicking a remote control button, the user activates the link and a new multimedia object is displayed.

The application for GINGA Middleware was developed in NCL language using NCL Eclipse [16] as a tool. It has non-linear content, in which all the objects are synchronized with each other including the audio and the main video. The development shows how the objects are structured and related in space and time.

Figure 3 shows the codes used to implement interactivity. These codes refer to the keys on the PC keyboard that allow simulating the TV remote control buttons in Ginga Windows.

The remote control	●	●	●	●
Windows Keys	F1	F2	F3	F4
NCL code	RED	GREEN	YELLOW	BLUE

Fig. 3. Ginga-Windows codes used to simulate the remote control

The objective of the interactive content in this case was to encourage reflection on the amount of plastic used daily, the garbage generated and the consequences for the environment.

In general, viewers take decisions based on their previous knowledge or understanding of the information provided. For this reason, instead of the usual option menu, the interactivity was incorporated depending on the argument. This is illustrated in Fig. 4, which shows a point of entry to a path of the hyper-content that leads from Video 1 to Video 2 (Fig. 2). The interactivity- associated argument was represented as a blue text box with white letters, which the viewer selects by pressing the blue button on the remote control (simulated by F4 in Windows).

Fig. 4. Interactivity-associated argument is represented as a text box with a question on blue background. (Color figure online)

4   Reconstruction and Analysis of Interactive Processes

To develop a pedagogical model for educational uses of iDTV, knowledge about how we interact in such environments is essential. We therefore first aimed to explore interactions with an iDTV application.

The interpretative study of an activity should be based on the discursive dimension of the situation. The dialogic nature of discourse, including digital discourse, enables a detailed analysis of the phenomenon that occurs in representation and meaning processes. This kind of analysis uses an interactional time scale [17] that represents information granularity, with a short time span of minutes or seconds, and allows considering digital interaction.

Interactivity allows for content personalization based on the users´ decisions (where they want to go) within the limits imposed by the design. The narrative dimension appears in the interaction—it develops in time following a linear operations chain that triggers a succession of states. In this dimension, the user manipulates virtual objects (texts, images, sounds, etc.) until achieving the expected result, and generates different system states at each stage [4].

An instrument is proposed for the exploration of discourse components in an interactive session with an iDTV application. The reconstruction and analysis of the viewer's narrative takes into account the conceptual, social, and technological dimensions of interaction. The digital one considers the characteristics of the devices used, the narratives offered, and the interaction sequences developed by viewers. It also deals with the disturbances regarding the application or the content, which express the meaning attributed to the activity.

This instrument was designed with a learning situation in mind, in which the viewer interacts with an iDTV application. Its content has local interactivity; the viewer accesses the data received and stored in the set-top-box.

The record of the actions performed on screen and of the audios and videos, provides information on the interactive processes. At the end of the session, semi-structured interviews are carried out to keep a record of the viewer's perceptions of the usability of the application, and the viewer's comprehension level of the content delivered.

4.1   Methodology for the Analysis of Interactions. A Case Study Description

One pilot study was implemented to identify the navigation features associated with the construction of a narrative. Since the content was related to information on the environment which may be of interest to children, young people and adults, potential viewers were estimated to be of a wide range of ages. Ten participants of different ages, occupations and interests were selected for the analysis. They all had experience using interactive technology. Interestingly, some of them were consumers of YouTube videos and video games. Table 1 shows the participants and their characteristics.

Two different versions of the application were used for the interactions test. In the first version, interactivity points were indicated by button icons representing the

Table 1. List of participants' characteristics (age, occupation/interests)

Participant	Age	Occupation/interests	Interactive experiences
T1	75	Housewife	Internet
T2	9	Primary school student	Internet, YouTube, Videogames
T3	24	Graduate in business administration	internet, social networks, videogames, YouTube
T4	21	Environmental technology student	internet, social networks, videogames, YouTube
T5	25	Lawyer	internet, social networks, YouTube
T6	35	Bank employee	internet, social networks
T7	38	Systems engineer	internet, e-mail, social networks
T8	48	Physics secondary teacher	internet, e-mail, social networks
T9	18	New entrant to university	internet, social networks, videogames, YouTube
T10	41	Primary teacher	internet, social networks

concepts to be explored. In the second one, they were indicated by a question in a text box. In both versions, interactive elements were accessed through the blue button on the remote control. Table 3 indicates the version with which each participant interacted (* = icons, and ✓ = text box).

For data collection, the PC Ginga-Windows simulator was used and all digital and dialogic interactive sequences were recorded. Freez Screen Video Capture software allowed us to record the screen actions and audio of the interaction—in this case, oral comments by the viewers while they interacted with the application. The interviews with each viewer were also recorded in audio format. Events occurred with the passage of time, at the beginning or end of the playback of multimedia objects and following the viewer's actions on the remote control.

4.2   Reconstruction and Interpretation of Narratives

Being an exploratory study, this first approach shows the structure of the narrative created by the viewers, and their opinions on the subject and the application. We believe this will allow reconstructing their experience and understanding their particular ways of creating paths. In other words, the idea is to recreate a process of knowledge representations and retrievals.

To do this, we first need to know possible navigation paths designed for the application. The application interface uses visual language that integrates formal vocabulary and syntax that describes and controls the system elements. As Fig. 2 shows, content navigation may be the following:

- Linear, without user's interaction. The main content is presented in video format (*V1*) with an explicit time limit (-●). In this route, the objects displayed are activated to follow links to other information nodes. Dotted lines with diamonds at the ends (◆....◆) indicate intervals in which interactivity is activated.

- First level hyper navigation, with user interaction. The main content is developed in video format (*V1*), and objects displayed in image format offer two interactivity points. The images are blue text boxes with questions inviting the user to explore the concepts, associated with the blue button on the remote control (*Plastic Bags and Garbage*). By clicking on these objects, the user starts playback of videos (*V2*) and (*V5*) respectively, both with an explicit time limit.
- Second level hyper navigation, with user interaction. Access to information nodes is allowed only if the nodes in the previous level have been accessed before. In the example, during video playback (*V2*) two new interactivity points are indicated by image objects. Images are blue text boxes with new questions (*Time, Bottle*). As in the previous level, interactivity is associated with the blue button on the remote control. By clicking on the objects, the user starts playback of videos (*V3*) and (*V4*) respectively, both with an explicit time limit.

A description is offered of how data are constructed by integrating the conceptual categories with the above-mentioned records.

The analysis of an interactive session with an iDTV application, helps us identify actions that modify the development of the activity and generate changes in the way the user approaches the object—e.g. selection of complementary content, gaps in the interactive sequence, execution of nodes in parallel, etc. Such actions, called disturbances, allow fragmenting data into a group of interaction segments (IS). Table 2 shows possible actions to be carried out on content with interactivity based on navigation options. The interpretative analysis of the segments allows inferring each user's work style.

In the case of this application, the IS can only be started through disturbances related to SA (start of the activity) and NN (opening of a new information node).

Table 2. Interaction disturbances that determine fragmentation.

Code	Disturbance	Description	Possible examples
SA	Start of activity	The first interaction segment is started	
CS	Change of scene	A new scene is uploaded resulting in a screen change. This disturbance occurs when it is possible to fast-forward or rewind the recording.	The scene "n: < En>" is selected
NN	New Node	A new complementary node is opened. This disturbance takes place when there are several simultaneous options, for example in the case of an option menu.	An image object is enlarged A video object is enlarged An text object is enlarged
NP	New node in parallel	A new node in parallel is opened. Several parallel contents are displayed on the same screen—for example a video with an accompanying text.	The situation is presented from a different perspective

By interacting with the content, each viewer creates a personal narrative depending on previous experience with multimedia applications. Table 3 shows the narratives created by the 10 participants in the interaction test. The nodes selected by the participants are indicated in blue.

Table 3. Narratives created by the 10 participants through content interaction

Viewer	Navigation sequence
T1 (✓)	V1-**V5**-V1
	V1-**V2**-V1-**V5**-V1
	V1-**V2**-**V3**-V2-**V4**-V2-V1-**V5**-V1
T2 (✓)	V1
	V1-**V2**-**V4**-V2-V1-**V5**-V1
	V1-**V2**-**V3**-V2-**V4**-V2-V1-**V5**-V1
T3 (✓)	V1-**V2**-**V4**-V2-V1-**V5**-V1
	V1
	V1-**V2**-**V3**-V2-**V4**-V2-(exit)
T4 (✓)	V1-**V2**-V1-**V5**-V1
	V1-**V2**-**V3**-V2-V1
	V1-**V2**-**V4**-V2-V1
T5 (✓)	V1-**V5**-V1
	V1-**V2**-**V3**-V2-**V4**-V2-V1-**V5**-V1
T6 (✓)	V1-**V5**-V1
	V1-**V2**-**V4**-V2-V1-**V5**-V1
T7 (*)	V1-**V5**-V1
	V1-**V2**-**V4**-V2-V1
T8 (*)	V1
	V1-**V2**-V1-**V5** (exit)
	V1-**V2**-V1 (exit)
	V1-**V2**-**V3**-V2-**V4**-V2-V1-**V5**-V1
T9 (*)	V1-**V5**-V1
	V1-**V2**-**V3**-V2-V1-**V5**-V1
	V1-**V2**-**V3**-V2-**V4**-V2-V1-exit
T10 (*)	V1-**V5**-V1
	V1-**V2**-**V3**-V2-**V4**-V2-V1-**V5**-V1

Some participants considered only the V1 linear content sequence. This narrative was observed for participants T2 and T8 when they first dealt with the content.

Participants who navigated the whole content followed the sequence V1-**V2**-**V3**-V2-**V4**-V2-V1-**V5**-V1. Nodes accessed by choice are indicated in bold; access to node V2 by default, after accessing second level nodes **V3** and **V4** (see Fig. 5), is indicated in italics.

It should be noted that none of the participants carried out a complete navigation (that is, visited all the nodes) the first time they interacted with the content.

Two participants visited all the nodes in the second trail, two in the third one, one in the fourth, and three participants, two of whom used "exit" not to revisit nodes, did so in different paths. Thus eight participants in total carried out a complete navigation.

Six participants accessed **V5** video node (see Fig. 2) in the first interaction with the content—narrative V1-**V5**-V1. Three of them reported not seeing the icon that indicates access to V2 node (Plastic Bag). On a second visit, and after being advised of the presence of interactive objects, they accessed V2 node, and second level nodes V3 and V4. Other participants said that they had tried to access to V2 but had not been successful. For example T7 explained that image delivery was too fast and so allowed no time to access the buttons or to read the instructions displayed at the beginning.

In general, participants had difficulty in identifying interactivity points. All of them expressed interest in some issues regarding the subject matter. However, none of them were interested in the interactive features of the videos.

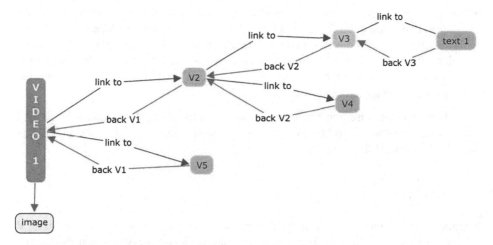

Fig. 5. Diagram of a navigation sequence. Links selected by the viewer are indicated in blue, and a red line indicates the video sequences determined by context default. (Color figure online)

Interactive processes between viewers and content can be regarded as cultural communication processes. An interaction can then be considered as an interchange of meaning and representations—a representation of a particular object can be generated from stimuli such as meaningful dots, strokes or sounds.

5   Results and Discussion

The variety of stimuli and languages is certainly relevant when considering the viewer's representations which are of course not necessarily the same as those of the content designer. At this stage, an interesting result is obtained from the viewers' statements regarding the representations fostered by the content, and the presentation and usability of such content.

It should be noted that all viewers played the video two or three times and these different recreations are understood as instances of content recovery. The first time, none of them identified the possibility of examining some specific ideas. This was probably due to the viewer's representation of what we call "button" which becomes evident here. By "button" we usually mean that which allows choosing a concept to be further explored (for example, bags). From the point of view of the image presented, in this case that button was a text box with a question. At the beginning of the video, participants were told they would have to press certain computer keys (that simulated the buttons on a remote control) associated with particular colors. The representation of a button proved therefore difficult.

In addition, the video introduces at the beginning a warning reading "Attention: this documentary is interactive". This seemed to make the participants feel the need to start running the file.

Some other observations emerged:

- When a link from one node to another is activated there is a discontinuity in the audio. This made participants wonder whether it had come to an end.
- After the story of contaminated food resulting from fish that eat bags, the audio asks, "Who eats this food?", and most viewers answered, "We do". We consider the tone of the question recreates that of a traditional class in which participants are prompted to complete a phrase with one word.

It is worth mentioning that a computer was used for the study. The keys (Ctrl + F) simulated the remote control buttons and this, as pointed out above, became an obstacle because it distorted the context.

6 Conclusion

Methodological guidelines for the analysis of interactions made by viewers of ITV content are presented in this work. It is expected to devise a pedagogical model that makes use of the potential of this technology to improve educational practices.

The proposed methodology is based on the reconstruction of the narratives of interaction from the actions on screen. The interactions are studied from the perspective of effectively "the person" running and interactions that would like to make, reflected in what they say as they interact.

Four possible disturbances were identified for iDTV content (Start of activity, Change of scene, New node, New node in parallel). In the tests with content designed ad hoc for this study, we identified Start of activity (SA) and New node (NN), based on which navigation sequences were reconstructed. New disturbances may occur depending on the interactivity possibilities of the content.

We suggest future studies into narratives that result from interactions with content offering more interactive possibilities, such as simultaneous navigation, playback control (play, pause, rewind, fast-forward) and hypertextual navigation. The idea is to consider more complex interactive designs that would allow implementing learning activities involving exploratory actions and activity management.

We also propose the use of Smart TV, and activities performed by pairs of viewers interacting with the content and with each other so that their dialogues could provide complementary information about actions on the screen.

To further explore interactions with iDTV content, we propose to search for the most effective strategy to define interaction intervals, and to study how viewers perceive the layout of content with interactivity points.

The development of a pedagogical model based on technology-mediated learning involves activities that promote interactions aimed. In the case of iDTV applications, the relationship between interactivity and pedagogical model is established in the content. The content should have enough interactivity to generate the necessary dialogic interactions between the learner and the application.

References

1. Lytras, M., Lougos, C., Chozos, P., Pouloudi, A.: Interactive television and e-learning convergence: examining the potential of t-learning. In: Proceedings of the European Conference on eLearning. Brunel, UK (2002)
2. Castañeda, L., Adell, J. (eds.): Entornos personales de aprendizaje: Claves para el ecosistema educativo en la red. Marfil, Alcoy (2013). http://www.um.es/ple/libro/
3. González, A., Jiménez, K.: La televisión digital interactiva y sus aplicaciones educativas [Interactive digital TV and its learning tools]. Comunicar **26**, 93–101 (2006)
4. Scolari, C.: Hacer Clic: Hacia una sociosemiótica de las interacciones digitales. Gedisa, Barcelona (2004)
5. Hernández, R., Morales, M., de la Roca, M.: Los desafíos del diseñador instruccional en el campo del t-Learning. In: Proceedings of I Jornadas de Difusión y Capacitación de Aplicaciones y Usabilidad de la Televisión Digital Interactiva jAUTI, pp. 104–111. La Plata (2012)
6. Abadía, I.: Revisión de lineamientos para el desarrollo de contenido educativo para televisión digital interactiva. Revista S&T **10**(20), 71–104 (2011)
7. Engeström, Y.: Activity theory and individual and social transformation. In: Engeström, Y., Miettinen, R., Punamäki, R. (eds.) Perspectives on Activity Theory, pp. 19–38. University Press, Cambridge (1992)
8. Perkins, D.N.: La persona-más. Una visión distribuida del pensamiento y el aprendizaje. In: Salomon, G. (ed.) Cogniciones distribuidas: Consideraciones psicológicas y educativas, pp. 126–154. Amorrortu, Buenos Aires (2001)
9. Rabardel, P.: People and Technology (2002). http://ergoserv.psy.univ-paris8.fr/
10. Zajc, M., Isteničstarčič, A.: Interactive multimedia t-learning environments: potential of DVB-T for learning. V: ISTENIČSTARČIČ, A. (ur.), ŠUBIC KOVAČ, M. (ur.). University & industry knowledge transfer and innovation. Athens [etc.]: WSEAS Press, str, pp. 103–123 (2009)
11. Rabardel, P., Bourmaud, G.: From artefact to instrument. Interact. Comput. **15**, 665–669 (2003)
12. Santos, G., Miranda, A.: Interacciones en procesos educativos con tecnología. Algunas consideraciones para TVDi. In: Abásolo, M.J. (ed.) Anales de JAUTI 2012- I Jornadas Iberoamericanas de Difusión y Capacitación sobre Aplicaciones y Usabilidad de la Televisión Digital Interactiva. Universidad Nacional de La Plata, La Plata (2013)
13. Cuidemos el medio ambiente. Si vos haces tu parte, todos podemos, Facultad de Arte de la Universidad Nacional del Centro de la Provincia de Buenos Aires, Tandil, Argentina (2015). https://www.youtube.com/watch?v=81tcWKMhgGo

14. Aguirre, M.I.H.: Televisión digital: Contenidos interactivos y publicidad. Razón y Palabra, 73, pp. 1–7 (2010)
15. Arroyo, M., Schwartz, S., Cardozo, S., Tardivo, L.: CreaTVDigital: Composición Visual de Aplicaciones Interactivas para TV Digital. In: 41JAIIO - SSI, ISSN: 1850–2830, pp. 305-32. La Plata (2012). http://41jaiio.sadio.org.ar/SSI_Contribuciones
16. Azevedo, R.G.A., Neto, C.S.S., Teixeira, M.M., Santos, R.C.M., Gomes, T.A.: Textual authoring of interactive digital tv applications. In: Proceddings of the 9th International Interactive Conference on Interactive Television (EuroITV 2011), pp. 235–244. ACM, New York (2011)
17. Badreddine, Z., Buty, C.: Discursive reconstruction of the scientific story in a teaching sequence. Int. J. Sci. Edu. **33**(6), 773–795 (2011)

Audiovisual Accessibility

Accesibility on VoD Platforms via Mobile Devices

Ángel García-Crespo, José Luis López-Cuadrado,
and Israel González-Carrasco$^{(\boxtimes)}$

Computer Science Department, Universidad Carlos III de Madrid,
Av.de La Universidad 30, 28911 Leganés, Madrid, Spain
acrespo@ia.uc3m.es, {jllopez,igcarras}@inf.uc3m.es

Abstract. At present, the fast and constant evolution of intelligent terminals and mobile platforms is opening a new world of possibilities and applications that can meet many of the different needs human beings face in their daily lives. It is in the field of accessibility where new technologies can have a real impact, offering new means and alternatives to access the information around us. Modern-day society enjoys a wide range of cultural possibilities everyone can choose from, but persons with auditory and/or visual impairment have problems accessing them. This article presents the WhatsCine system, a system conceived to foster inclusion, shared leisure and equal access to culture for everyone, for the particular case of VOD platforms.

Keywords: Audio-visual accessibility · Captions · Audiodescription · Sign language · Video on demand

1 Introduction

The term accessibility has been associated almost exclusively and for quite some time with the mobility of the body and the disappearance of physical barriers [1]. But this conception of accessibility has become obsolete with the constant advances in accessing what is increasingly globalized and omnipresent information. In this day and age, accessibility implies the integration not only of people with physical disabilities, but also those with sensory deficiencies. The proliferation of media that transmit information, such as cinema, television, DVDs and the Internet as its chief exponent, along with other types of events such as theater, opera and conferences, elevates access to this volume of information to a basic right for all people.

The importance of this right is such that the United Nations recognizes it in its International Convention on the Rights of People with Disabilities, approved December 13th, 2006 and ratified in Spain in the Congress of Deputies on October 18th, 2007. Noteworthy is article 30, which categorically affirms that nations must adopt all pertinent measures to assure that disabled people have access to television programs, films, theatre and other cultural activities in accessible formats [2].

Usually video contents are delivered by TV channels. There are users, as elder people or people with disabilities, who cannot access said video contents it due to the

© Springer International Publishing Switzerland 2016
M.J. Abásolo et al. (Eds.): jAUTI 2015/CTVDI 2015, CCIS 605, pp. 149–160, 2016.
DOI: 10.1007/978-3-319-38907-3_12

lack of accessibility elements. According to Moreno et al., there is a set of barriers both in the content and in the user agent [3].

It is within this context that the WhatsCine system can be applied since the main goal of the system is to offer alternative methods of accessing information about any kind of cultural event or show, making it easier to follow, for example, the plot of a film or a play script at the same time it is being acted out.

Alternative means of offering this information might be very different depending on the type of event or the type of disability in question, but, although the UN Convention does not specify what practices must be undertaken to introduce accessible formats, there is a general consensus about the most common methods necessary to make information accessible:

- Audio description for the blind and for persons with visual impairment.
- Subtitles for the deaf and for people with hearing impairment.
- Representation with sign language.

This is why the WhatsCine system was conceived and developed with the goal of offering these three ways of communication at any kind of show or cultural event.

This article describes the purpose of the WhatsCine system and how it works in the following sections. Section 2 discusses the solutions that exist right now for dealing with the problems that WhatsCine also tries to solve. Section 3 presents the general architecture of the system so that one can more easily understand how it works. Section 4 describes detailed uses of the application, and Sect. 5 presents the VoD accessibility project. Lastly, Sect. 6 presents some conclusions about the project.

2 State of the Art

As mentioned in the previous section, nations must adopt all pertinent measures to assure that disabled people have access to television programs, films, theatre and other cultural activities in accessible formats [2]. People with disabilities has the right to access video contents and they are mobilizing online to advocate for better television accessibility [4]. Organizations like CNSE (Confederación Estatal de Personas Sordas), FIAPAS (Federación Ibérica de Asociaciones de Padres y Amigos de los Sordos) and ONCE (Organización Nacional de Ciegos Españoles) in Spain, EBU (European Blind Union) or EUD (European Union of the Deaf) at European level, as well as other many assotiations, at local, national and international level (as the World Blind Union or the World Federation of the Deaf), work in improve the accessibility of contents for people with disabilities.

Although it is perhaps now when, thanks to the possibilities of new technologies, more advances are being made in the field of audio-visual accessibility, such difficulties have in fact addressed beforehand. Solutions in audio description, subtitling and sign language have been on the market for some time, but in always different forms. WCAG 2.0 guidelines remarks the importance of accessibility for multimedia content, remarking the importance of including captions, audio description and sign language transcription for video accessibility [5] an provide a set of techniques to be applied [6].

As the goal of audio description is to provide a brief audio description of what is happening at an event, there must always be a transmitting element of the audio description itself and user devices that receive the sound. Audio description is very important in order to transmit emotions to the visually impaired [7]. The voice of audio description can be generated by text-to-speech techniques or using human voices [8]. The traditional approach has been to equip the theatre with a radio frequency system which transmits analogically to customers' devices. The main problem with these systems is that they are too expensive to implement on a large scale, and because it is an analog transmission, the level of sound can at times be too bothersome, especially in lengthy sessions.

The roots of subtitling are in the world of television, where, especially thanks to teletext initially, it was easy to subtitle any program, and with the latest advances it is also possible to include subtitles at live events [9]. The presentation of subtitles on a screen must meet a series of standards to facilitate the reading and comprehension of what is being shown on the screen [10, 11]. However, in reality, the application of subtitling techniques is far from uniform, because despite the existence of standards [12–14], each organization tends to apply its own, lacking consistency and making mistakes of implementation which often give rise to spelling errors, speeds that are difficult to follow or the appearance of too many lines of information. Standards also depends on the country where they are applied and its corresponding laws. Despite we cite Spanish references, other authors like Packer et al. reviews history, benefits and guidelines for video description in USA [15]. WhatsCine can bring uniformity to this field since it treats all subtitling information in a coherent, esthetically correct way. Some captioning approaches explore the real time captioning to be applied in several areas like health-care [16].

The WhatsCine system is also of great help in the expansion and use of sign language. To make an event accessible through sign language, it is always necessary to have an interpreter who performs at the same time the event is happening if it is live, or who appears on a screen if the event is recorded, as in a film. In the first case, the interpreter must always be available for the successive occasions the event is repeated. In the second case, all the spectators have to see the interpretation of the sign language on the screen whether they need to or not. WhatsCine makes it possible for the interpretation to be performed always when necessary and only for people who are really interested in it. Other sign language approaches are based on the automatic interpretation of the speech [17]. However, the implementation of said techniques is complex for being included in a solution like the presented in this paper. Using virtual interpreters is another cost effective approach [18], based on the recognition of the language of the video and there are many approaches in several languages like Italian [19] or Spanish [20]. This kind of techniques could ease the process of generating sign language translations to be included as accessibility element for films.

3 System Architecture

Before explaining the uses of the WhatsCine system, it is helpful to have a broader view of the system's general architecture to understand its functioning and display. The design of the system makes it easy to set up compared with other, more expensive solutions that rely on equipment that is more difficult to acquire and distribute at shows and events. Figure 1 depicts an overview of WhatsCine's architecture and the main components of the system are shown.

WhatsCine works using Internet as a channel of communication with a central server that provides coverage to everyone who wishes to use it. This server is the main component of the system, containing the software necessary to manage the elements of accessibility by containing such elements: audio description, subtitles and sign language videos. It also manages synchronization with customers to indicate what moment the reproduction is at and show everyone the same content simultaneously.

Each user connects to the accessibility server through personal mobile devices. These terminals receive the audio of the audio description, the video with the sign language and the content of the subtitles, all synchronized, via the wireless network. The advantage of the customer terminals is that it will be the users' own intelligent devices (smartphones and tablets) that function as such, making the introduction of the WhatsCine system even more viable. The mobile platforms that WhatsCine has been designed for are iOS and Android. Among the reasons why both systems were chosen is that, between them, they hold approximately 90 % of the market share. Anyone who has an intelligent phone or tablet is almost completely assured to have one of the two operating systems, which increases the compatibility that WhatsCine can have even more. It also eliminates the need for the organization or company handling the accessibility of the show or event to provide these customer terminals.

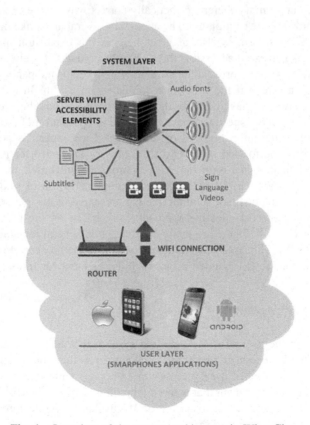

Fig. 1. Overview of the system architecture in WhatsCine

4   Accessibility Options to be Offered

Users enter the elements of accessibility through the main menu of the app.

In the proposed case of study, choosing the DEMO option accesses the film catalogue (see Fig. 2).

Fig. 2. Initial screen of WhatsCine with all the available options

Fig. 3. Films available in the catalogue

In Fig. 3 the user can select a film within the available catalogue. When one of the films is selected, the accessibility options available for it appear (see Fig. 4).

The three main uses of the system are conveniently labelled within the customer application (Fig. 4). Hence, end users could choose between three accessibility elements available in WhatsCine for each film of the catalogue: subtitles, audiodescription or sign language. To synchronize these accessibility elements WhatsCine captures the audio of the film for short time and then it send it to the server. In the server, this audio is checked in order to determine the current time of the movie.

For example, a person who wishes to access the audio description only needs to pass a finger over the screen of the device to know which option they are in, and pressing twice will confirm the choice. In Fig. 5, there is an example of the synchronize screen. The user has to put the finger over the screen (in Spanish: "Pulse aquí para Sincronizar") and the audio of the film will be captured and used to synchronize the

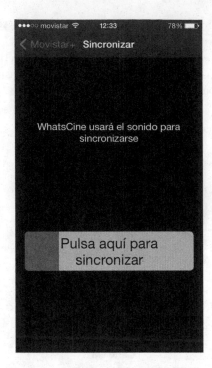

Fig. 4. Selection of accessibility elements for each film of the catalogue.

Fig. 5. Synchronize screen in WhatsCine.

audiodescription and the current position of the movie. Blind users are guided by the screen reader they use.

Of course, not all events require all the modes of accessibility. If, for example, only the option of audio description and subtitles is configured in the server, the sign language feature will not appear on the terminal.

Once the desired element of accessibility is chosen, it is downloaded onto the device and stored to be accessed from the download tab.

With the film on the TV, pressing the tab will start the synchronization with the central server.

4.1 Audio Description

Audio description consists fundamentally of providing audio information about all the data, situations and details essential for understanding certain works, functions and events, cultural or any other type, that only appear visually [11]. The introduction of WhatsCine in places such as movie theatres might help audio description reach places and media where it has not had much success, thus establishing it as a common feature. Moreover, it makes it possible to receive audio description without needing a special device (like an FM receiver), so one can listen to the audio description from one's own personal device without interfering with the sound in the rest of the theatre.

To access the audio description, the user must insert their earphones so that this way only they can listen to it without disturbing other spectators nearby.

4.2 Subtitles

The goal of subtitles is to show dialogues, translated or not, of a scene from a film or play, along with important information that can indicate other sounds in the scene. What makes subtitling unique is that it can be used not only to help persons with hearing impairment follow a play or a film, but also for situations where it is necessary to present information apart from the visual content or when it is necessary to show the conversations of actors or the talk of a speaker in a language different from one's own. Like the audio description, the subtitles are also configured in the interface of the server's software. In this interface, the files that have the subtitles must be specified along with the name that will appear in the interface of the customer application.

An important aspect to keep in mind about subtitles is the format they must be in to be stored in the server and shown properly in the customer applications. The applications, in iOS as well as in Android, read these files and they appear on the device at the speed the server indicates. The subtitles are contained in XML files according to the film projection standard Digital Cinema Package (DCP) [8]. DCP represents the compressed and encoded file or group of files that contain the content and information associated with a film or a short. It is possible to find more information about this standard at the following reference.

The user selects a subtitle language that corresponds to a file stored in the server. The customer applications download read that file, interpret it, and ask the server what moment the session is at, and have a timer which shows the subtitles read as time elapses. To synchronize the subtitles, WhatsCine captures the audio of the film for short time and then it send it to the server. In the server, this audio is checked in order to determine the current time of the movie. The customer periodically checks the time of the event with the server and makes sure the subtitles are being shown properly to avoid synchronization errors that might be bothersome and impede understanding.

Fig. 6. Display of subtitles in WhatsCine

In Fig. 6 there is an example of the display of subtitles in the screen of the mobile device. The display of subtitles is synchronized with the audio of the film. Within the subtittle accessibility element, if the user want to re-synchronize the subtitles could use the option synchronize available in the menu.

4.3   Sign Language

Sign language is the last option of accessibility the system offers and is also geared toward users with hearing impairment, as it establishes a channel of communication through which these people can receive and understand the dialogues and conversations that take place in a specific scene.

As is done with subtitles, it is necessary to configure the sign language options in the server. In the server, the video file that contains the recording of the interpreter making the signs and the language the signs are made in must be specified so that users can clearly choose one or another in the interface of the customer application.

The procedure with sign language videos is the same as with subtitles. The video file is downloaded to the customer applications and next the audio captured with WhatsCine is sent to the server (as with the Synchronize option of Fig. 5). Then, the server is asked how many seconds have elapsed since the session began to set the reproduction to the moment it is at. From that point, the reproduction will continue without interruption for as long as the user wants.

Fig. 7. Display of sign language in WhatsCine

All that appears on the screen of the device is the video with the interpreter, as shown in Fig. 7. The video is synchronized with the audio of the film. Within the sign language accessibility element, if the user want to re-synchronize the video could use the option synchronize available in the menu.

5   Case of Study

One of the problems of VoD platforms is their inclusion of elements of accessibility. Although in many countries it is not legally mandatory to make elements of accessibility accessible, it should, however, be a moral obligation. In the United States, the Americans with Disabilities Act requires new audiovisual Internet content to have closed captioning. One of the main distributors of VoD, Netflix, faces the problem that all players which can reproduce Netflix must be enabled for closed captioning.

The inclusion of closed captions covers only one segment of persons with sensory disability. It completely neglects blind persons, as it does not include audio description, and much of the deaf community, which needs sign language for good communication.

Given the potential of WhatsCine to make audiovisual content accessible, the system is being used to make the Movistar + cinema offer accessible.

As it is a totally innovative experience, in addition to including accessibility elements in the platform, a global communication project has been developed together with follow-up of user satisfaction. For that purpose, all persons in Spain with hearing and/or visual impairment have been invited to access a microsite designed for this purpose, www.televisionaccessible.com, to learn about the experience first-hand and help improve it by leaving their opinions and suggestions.

The aim is to launch the first totally accessible television and make the mentioned TV platform the pay television with the best video offer for all users in Spain. Since August 2015, the Movistar + platform has been offering films in accessible format via the WhatsCine application at no additional cost, as the price of the rental does not change.

Any person, customer of the VoD channel or not, can access www.television accessible.com and view the video demonstration to learn how the app works, try it with demo films and leave comments. There are also answers to frequently asked questions in this section. The company will raffle a pack consisting of a smartphone, a tablet and a smart TV. The drawing will be open to anyone giving opinions and suggestions on the microsite.

After the pilot finishes, a group of persons chosen by CNSE (Confederación Estatal de Personas Sordas), FIAPAS (Federación Ibérica de Asociaciones de Padres y Amigos de los Sordos) and ONCE (Organización Nacional de Ciegos Españoles) will carry out user tests to confirm the experience is adapted to their needs and to suggest improvements for future versions of the app (Fig. 8).

People with hearing impairment have the option of choosing between Spanish Sign Language (initalled LES in Spanish) in addition to dialogue transcripts, provide(s) the identification of characters via colors, information about sounds and the intonation of the dialogues. Neither the LSE interpreter nor the subtitles are visualized on the TV screen but instead appear on the user's smartphone or tablet (Fig. 9).

So that people with hearing impairment can more freely enjoy the elements of accessibility, the researchers have patented a special stand that makes it possible to view the subtitles and sign language at the same time as the audiovisual elements in an environment of augmented reality (Figs. 8 and 9).

Fig. 8. Stand with multi-language subtitles

Fig. 9. Stand with sign language and subtitles.

Likewise, persons with visual impairment can use the audio description system, which works via earphones connected to a smartphone or tablet.

How does WhatsCine work with the proposed VoD channel? To watch accessible cinema, it is necessary to:

- Download and install the free WhatsCine app from Play Store or Apple Store on one's Android or iOS smartphone or tablet.
- Access the app from the device and select the options WIFI or 3G.
- Click on name of the VoD channel to know what films are available on the grid and choose one.

- Choose the kind of accessibility needed: audio description, subtitles or sign language. Just press the one chosen and begin the download.
- Activate and synchronize the accessibility in the downloads section to watch the film.

From this moment, the application is completely synchronized with the television and the user can pause as often as they want, rewind, fast forward, or stop it and resume it later at the exact point where they left off.

At the end of the pilot the pilot a lessons learned analysis as well as a user evaluation. The user evaluation should cover usability elements, quality of the content deployed, technology acceptance, user experience and suggestion of improvements. Evaluation results will provide feedback about the points to be improved, specially for the user experience and technology acceptance aspects, because they are important issues for people with sensory disabilities.

6 Conclusions

The system presented in this article aspires to contribute a solution to the world of accessibility and integration of the hearing and/or visually impaired into society and culture. Because it is based on personal mobile devices, the solution eliminates the need for more complex technical alternatives, taking advantage of the current promotion of intelligent telephones and tablets.

WhatsCine offers an economically and materially viable way of introducing a system of accessibility based on audio description, subtitling and sign language. This system establishes new channels of communication between content creators and artists (directors, actors, speakers, etc.) and all users who wish to access this content regardless of their condition. It thus breaks down a long-existing barrier, but which can be overcome with systems such as this one.

References

1. Cintas, J.D.: La accesibilidad a los medios de comunicación audiovisual a través del subtitulado y la audiodescripción. In: González, L., Hernúñez, P. (eds.) Cooperación y Diálogo. Esletra, Madrid (2010). (in Spanish)
2. United Nations' Convention on the Rights of Persons with Disabilities. http://www.un.org/disabilities/convention/conventionfull.shtml (Accessed 13 January 2016)
3. Moreno, L., Gonzalez, M., Martínez, P., Iglesias, A.: A Study of Accessibility Requirements for Media Players on the Web. In: Stephanidis, C. (ed.) Universal Access in HCI, Part I, HCII 2011. LNCS, vol. 6765, pp. 249–257. Springer, Heidelberg (2011)
4. Ellis, K.: Netflix closed captions offer an accessible model for the streaming video industry, but what about audio description? Commun. Politics Cult. **47**(3), 3–20 (2015)
5. Caldwell, B. et al.: Web Content Accessibility Guidelines 2.0, World Wide Web Consortium (W3C) recommendation, April 2008. https://www.w3.org/TR/WCAG20/

6. Techniques and Failures for Web Content Accessibility Guidelines 2.0, World Wide Web Consortium (W3C) Working Group Note, 26 February 2015. https://www.w3.org/TR/WCAG20-TECHS/

7. Ramos, M.: The emotional experience of films: does audio description make a difference? Translator **21**(1), 68–94 (2015)

8. Fernández i Torné, A., Matamala, A.: Text-to-speech vs. human voiced audio descriptions. J. Specialised Trans., JosTrans **24**, 0061–0088 (2015)

9. García-Crespo, A., González-Carrasco, I., López-Cuadrado, J.L., Ruiz-Mezcua, B.: Herramienta interactiva para la realización de la accesibilidad a eventos en Directo. In: Libro de actas DRT4ALL 2011 IV Congreso Internacional de Diseño, Redes de Investigación y Tecnología para todos, pp. 501–507, Fundación ONCE para la Cooperación e Inclusión Social de las Personas con Discapacidad, Madrid (2011) (in Spanish)

10. Rodriguez, A.M.P.: El subtitulado para sordos: estado de la cuestión en España. Quaderns: Rev. de Traducció **12**, 161–172 (2005)

11. Navarro, M.H., López, M.E.: Accessibilidad de la cultura visual: límites y perspectivas. Integración: Rev. sobre Ceguera y Deficiencia Vis. **40**, 21–28 (2002). (in Spanish)

12. UNE 153020. Audiodescripción para personas con discapacidad visual: requisitos para la audiodescripción y elaboración de audioguías. AENOR. Madrid (2005) (in Spanish)

13. UNE 153010:2012. Subtitulado para personas sordas y personas con discapacidad auditiva. Subtitulado a través de teletexto. AENOR, Madrid (2012) (in Spanish)

14. Digital Cinema System Specification, v.1.2. http://www.dcimovies.com/archives/spec_v1_2_No_Errata_Incorporated/DCIDigitalCinemaSystemSpecv1_2.pdf (Accessed 13 January 2016)

15. Packer, J., Vizenor, K., Miele, J.A.: An overview of video description: history, benefits, and guidelines. J. Vis. Impairment Blindness (Online) **109**(2), 83 (2015)

16. Spehar, B., Tye-Murray, N., Myerson, J., Murray, D.J.: Real-time captioning for improving informed consent: patient and physician benefits. Reg. Anesth. Pain Med. **41**(1), 65–68 (2016)

17. Boulares, M., Jemni, M.: Learning sign language machine translation based on elastic net regularization and latent semantic analysis. Artif. Intell. Rev., 1–22 (2016). doi:10.1007/s10462-016-9460-3

18. Kipp, M., Nguyen, Q., Heloir, A., Matthes, S.: Assessing the deaf user perspective on sign language avatars. In: The Proceedings of the 13th International ACM SIGACCESS Conference on Computers and Accessibility, pp. 107–114. ACM, October 2011

19. Lombardo, V., Nunnari, F., Damiano, R.: A virtual interpreter for the Italian sign language. In: Safonova, A. (ed.) IVA 2010. LNCS, vol. 6356, pp. 201–207. Springer, Heidelberg (2010)

20. Baldassarri, S., Cerezo, E., Royo-Santas, F.: Automatic Translation System to Spanish Sign Language with a Virtual Interpreter. In: Gross, T., Gulliksen, J., Kotzé, P., Oestreicher, L., Palanque, P., Prates, R.O., Winckler, M. (eds.) INTERACT 2009. LNCS, vol. 5726, pp. 196–199. Springer, Heidelberg (2009)

Author Index

Printed in the United States
By Bookmasters

Printed in the United States
By Bookmasters